梦与莲花

——泰戈尔浪漫诗选

【印】泰戈尔 著　冰心 等 译

江苏凤凰科学技术出版社·南京

图书在版编目（CIP）数据

　　梦与莲花：泰戈尔浪漫诗选：汉英对照／（印）泰戈尔著；冰心等译．— 南京：江苏凤凰科学技术出版社，2015.11（2022.5重印）
　　（易人外语）
　　ISBN 978-7-5537-5472-7

　　Ⅰ．①梦… Ⅱ．①泰… ②冰… Ⅲ．①英语－阅读教学－自学参考资料②诗集－印度－现代 Ⅳ．① H319.4：I

中国版本图书馆 CIP 数据核字 (2015) 第 230826 号

易人外语
梦与莲花——泰戈尔浪漫诗选

著　　　者	【印】泰戈尔
译　　　者	冰　心 等
责 任 编 辑	祝　萍
责 任 监 制	方　晨
出 版 发 行	江苏凤凰科学技术出版社
出版社地址	南京市湖南路1号A楼，邮编：210009
出版社网址	http://www.pspress.cn
印　　　刷	天津丰富彩艺印刷有限公司
开　　　本	880 mm × 1 230 mm　1/32
印　　　张	10
字　　　数	140 000
版　　　次	2015年11月第1版
印　　　次	2022年5月第3次印刷
标 准 书 号	ISBN 978-7-5537-5472-7
定　　　价	45.00元

图书如有印装质量问题，可随时向我社印务部调换。

前言

拉宾德拉纳特·泰戈尔是印度的著名诗人、文学家、哲学家、社会活动家和印度民族主义者。1913年，他凭借诗集《吉檀迦利》获得诺贝尔文学奖。他的诗在印度享有史诗的地位，其代表作有《吉檀迦利》、《飞鸟集》、《眼中沙》、《家庭与世界》、《园丁集》、《新月集》、《文明的危机》等。

泰戈尔是世界文学史上的巨匠，写下了50多部诗集，被尊称为"诗圣"。此外，他还完成了12部中长篇小说、100多篇短篇小说、20多部剧本等大量作品，著作颇丰，他的作品被很多人们当作是"精神生活的灯塔"。

泰戈尔是中国读者心目中最具地位的外国作家之一，他的诗风对中国现代文学产生过重大影响，郭沫若、徐志摩、冰心等人都不同程度地受到了他的启迪。冰心早期的创作受泰戈尔的影响较大，她曾经说："我自己写《繁星》和《春水》的时候，并不是在写诗，只是受了泰戈尔的《飞鸟集》的影响，把许多'零碎的思想'，收集在一个集子里而已。"

泰戈尔深受西方浪漫主义影响，是一位具有浪漫主义风格的诗人，在他的众多抒情诗中，浪漫主义成分较重。他的诗歌不仅格调清新、诗句秀丽，还具有奇特的想像、优美的韵律和浓郁的抒情气息。他的诗歌总是弥漫着一种恬淡、飘逸的意境，能唤起人们对大自然、人类以及世界上美好事物的喜爱。

本书共分为5卷，分别为"仙人世界"、"莲花"、"旅途"、"女人如梦"以及"地牢"。书中收录了泰戈尔的《飞鸟集》《流萤集》《园丁集》《吉檀迦利》《新月集》和《采果集》，撷取了这6部诗集中的浪漫而唯美的语句。本书中英文对照，中文部分大部分采用了冰心的译文，并在"热词天地"板块对部分重要的词汇作了注解。田园主题的水彩插图，不仅有大自然的清新、花朵的娇美，还有孩童的天真和少女的恬美，通过图与文字的结合，为读者营造出一片片浪漫唯美的天地。

泰戈尔的诗集使我们明白，生活中并不是缺少美，而是缺少发现美的眼睛。希望通过朗读一首首泰戈尔的浪漫诗篇，能让读者朋友们忘记烦恼，洗去身心的疲劳，让美好的世界展现在眼前，使生命中的每一天都能充满欢乐和光明，充满爱，使我们的心灵返回最初的纯净。

目录

第一卷　仙人世界

飞鸟集 / 6
流萤集 / 16
园丁集 / 26
My Paper Boat / 我的纸船 26
The Fair Before the Temple / 庙前的集会 30
The Workman's Little Daughter / 工人的小女儿 32
In May / 在五月天里 34
Listening / 静听 36
Gifts / 礼物 38
Turn Them Away I Cannot / 我不能回绝他们 40
The Young Prince Is to Pass by Our Door / 年轻的王子要从我们门前走过 44
She Is I / 她就是我 46
When I Go Alone to My Love-Tryst / 当我独赴幽会的时候 49
Let Your Work Be! Bride / 放下你的工作吧，我的新娘 51
Come as You Are / 你就这样地来吧 53
Come to My Lake / 到我的湖上来吧 56
I Did Not Come near You / 我没有走近你 59
吉檀迦利 / 62
Seashore / 海滨 62
Colored Toys / 彩色玩具 64
新月集 / 66
The Source / 来源 66
The Land of the Exile / 流放之地 68
Fairyland / 仙境 72
The Further Bank / 远岸 75
The Champa Flower / 金色花 78
采果集 / 82

第二卷　莲花

飞鸟集 / 84
流萤集 / 98
园丁集 / 106
Let None Go back Home, Brothers / 我们都不回家吧，兄弟们　106
O My Bird / 呵，我的鸟儿　108
I Was Walking by the Road / 我在路边行走　110
Our Love Is Simple as a Song / 我们的爱像歌曲一样地单纯　113
Her Name Is Ranjana / 她的名字是软遮那　115
When They Reach This Spot / 当她们走到这地点的时候　118
Why Did You Peep at Me？/ 你为什么偷地看我？　120
He Only Comes and Goes Away / 他只是来了又走了　122
Why Did He Choose to Come My Door？/ 他为什么特地来到我的门前？　124
Why There Is Madness in Your Eyes？/ 为什么你眼里带着疯癫？　126

吉檀迦利 / 128
Light / 光明　128
Clouds / 云彩　130
Roaming Cloud / 浮云　132
Lotus / 莲花　134

新月集 / 136
The Banyan Tree / 榕树　136

第三卷　旅途

飞鸟集 / 140
流萤集 / 152
园丁集 / 162
To-day Is the Festival of Phantoms / 今天是幻影的节日　162
I Know You, Modest Mendicant / 我懂得你，谦卑的乞丐　164
I Cannot Understand Them / 我不懂得　166
You Can Never Know It / 你永远不能了解它　168
Speak to Me / 对我说吧　170
You Are My Own / 你是我一个人的　172
If This Be True / 这是否真的　174
I Know Your Art / 我知道你的妙计　176
Why Does He Not Come？/ 他为什么不回来呢？　178
My Heart Is Given to the Many / 我的心是要给与许多人的　180
My Love / 我爱　182
I Am Tired / 我疲倦了　184
It Is Time to Come Home / 是回家的时候了　186
Reader / 读者　188

吉檀迦利 / 190
Parting Word / 别话　190
Journey / 旅途　192
If the Day Is Done / 假如一天已经过去了　196

采果集 / 198

第四卷 女人如梦

飞鸟集 / 200
流萤集 / 208
园丁集 / 220
Where Do You Hurry？/ 你急忙地要到哪里去呢？ 220
It Is Evening / 夜晚了 222
When I Come Again / 当我再来的时候 224
A Woman Is Like a Dream / 女人如梦 226
I Dare Not / 我不敢 228
Drunk, I Will Follow You / 醉汉，我要跟随你 232
Forgive This Pair of Sinners / 饶恕这一对罪人吧 236
Time Is Short / 时间是短暂的 238
If / 如果 240
Why Did You Single Me Out / 你为什么把我挑选出来 242
Free Me from Your Bonds / 把我从你的枷锁中放出来吧 244
The Gardener / 园丁 246
吉檀迦利 / 250
Tired Eyes / 倦眼 250
新月集 / 251
The Flower-School / 花的学校 251

第五卷 地牢

飞鸟集 / 254
流萤集 / 266
园丁集 / 274
I Forget / 我忘却了 274
I Know Not What You Thought of Me / 我不知道你怎样看待我 277
Beauty, Carved in Stone / 石头雕成的"美" 280
My Heart Longs for the Meeting with You / 我的心想望和你相见 282
I Have Not My Rose / 我没有了玫瑰 284
Here Is the Same Sky / 那边还是那个天空 286
My Bride and I / 我的新娘和我 290
O Death, My Death / 呵，死亡，我的死亡 293
I Come to Praise You / 我来颂赞你 295
The Image upon the Altar / 龛里的偶像 297
You Man of Riches / 你这富有的人 300
Must You Call Me？/ 你定要叫我么？ 302
Traveller / 行路人 304
My Love in a Former Life / 我前生的爱 306
Let the Parting Be Sweet / 让别离甜柔吧 308
The Would-Be Ascetic / 自称的苦行人 310
I Shall Never Be an Ascetic / 我永不会做一个苦行者 312
I Hunt for the Golden Stag / 我要追逐金鹿 314
吉檀迦利 / 316
Dungeon / 地牢 316

第一卷
仙人世界

飞鸟集

1

Listen, my heart, to the whispers[1] of the world with which it makes love to you.

热词天地
1.whisper ['wɪspə(r)] n. 低语；沙沙声

听，我的心呀，听那世界的低语，
这是它在向你示爱呀！

2

You smiled and talked to me of nothing and I felt that for this
I had been waiting long.

你微笑着,却不与我说话,而我觉得,
为此,我已等待太久。

3

Like the meeting of the seagulls and the waves we meet and come near.
The seagulls[1] fly off, the waves roll away and we depart.

热词天地

1. seagull ['siːgʌl] *n.* 海鸥
   fly off 飞出；飞速（或突然）地跑掉

我们的相遇相吸就如海鸥与波涛的相遇，
海鸥飞去，波涛翻逝，而我们也已分别。

4

This longing is for the one who is felt in the dark, but not seen in the day.

这渴望是为了那
在黑夜里感知，而在白天却未见的。

5

One sad voice has its nest among the ruins[1] of the years.
It sings to me in the night，"I loved you."

热词天地

1.ruins ['ruːɪnz] *n.* 遗迹（ruin 的复数形式）；废墟

一个忧郁的声音，筑巢于逝水流年中。
它在夜晚向我歌唱："我爱过你。"

6

Love! when you come
　　with the burning lamp of pain in your hand,
I can see your face and know you as bliss[1].

热词天地

1. bliss [blɪs] *n.* 极乐；天赐的福

爱情呀，当你来到，
手中举着点燃的痛苦之灯，
我能够看见你的脸，而且以你为幸福。

7

One word keep for me in thy[1] silence, O world,
when I am dead, "I have loved."

热词天地

1.try [ðaɪ] *pron.* 你的（古英语 thou 的所有格）

当我死去时，请在你的沉默中为我保留那句话，
噢世界，
"我曾经爱过。"

8

When I stand before thee[1] at the day's end
thou[2] shalt[3] see my scars and know
that I had my wounds and also my healing.

热词天地

1.thee [ðiː] *pron.* 你（古英语 thou 的宾格）
2.thou [ðaʊ] *pron.* 你；尔，汝（古时候的叫法，用作第二人称单数代词的主格）
3.shalt [ʃælt] *v.* 将要；应该（古英语中 shall 的第二人称单数一般现在时）

当我在那日子的尽头，站在您面前，
您将看见我的伤疤并了解
我有过伤疤，也有法治愈。

9

Some day I shall sing to thee in the sunrise of some other world,
"I have seen thee before in the light of the earth, in the love of man."

热词天地

some day 总有一天；将来有一天；来日

总有一天，我将在另一世界的晨光里对你歌唱：
"我曾在地球的光亮里，在人的爱意中，见过你。"

10

The prelude[1] of the night is commenced[2] in the music of the sunset,
in its solemn hymn to the ineffable[3] dark.

热词天地

1.prelude ['prelju:d] *n.* 前奏；序幕；前奏曲
2.commence [kə'mens] *v.* 开始；着手于
3.ineffable [ɪn'efəb(ə)l] *adj.* 不可言喻的；不应说出的；难以形容的

夜的序曲始于夕阳的乐章，
始于对难言黑暗的庄严赞歌。

11

That love can ever lose is a fact that we cannot accept as truth.

爱情注定失去,这是我们无法接受的事实。

12

Let this be my last word, that I trust thy love.

我相信你的爱,让这做我的遗言吧!

流萤集

1

Let me not grope in vain in the dark but keep my
mind still in the faith
that the day will break
and truth will appear
in its simplicity[1].

热词天地

1.simplicity [sɪmˈplɪsətɪ] *n.* 简单，朴素；质朴；天真

我不要在黑暗里徒然摸索，
而要让我的心始终坚信
长夜必会破晓，
真理必将显现
它素朴的面容。

2

Through the silent night
I hear the returning vagrant hopes of the morning
knock at my heart.

透过沉寂的夜，我听见
归来的游子对黎明的渴望，
敲打着我的心扉。

3

Mistakes live in the neighbourhood of truth
and therefore delude us.

当谬误在真理的隔壁时，
就往往会迷惑我们。

4

The butterfly counts not months but moments,
and has time enough.

蝴蝶用瞬间而非年月计算生命,
所以它永远美丽。

5

Let my love, like sunlight, surround you
and yet give you illumined freedom.

让我的爱化作阳光,围绕在你的周围,
然后赠与你绚烂的自由。

6

Mind's underground moths[1]
grow filmy wings
and take a farewell flight
in the sunset sky.

热词天地

1. moth [mɒθ] *n.* 飞蛾

心底的飞蛾，
长出了清透的翅膀，
在日落的天空，
做一次告别的飞翔。

7

Days are coloured bubbles
that float upon the surface of fathomless night.

白日是色彩斑斓的气泡,
在幽黑深夜的表面上漂浮。

8

My offerings are too timid to claim your remembrance,
and therefore you may remember them.

我的奉献如此羞涩,不敢渴求你的怀念,
或许正因如此,你才会将它记取。

9

Leave out my name from the gift
If it be a burden,
but keep my song.

如果我的名字成为一种负担，
请将它从这份礼物中抹去，
只留下我的欢歌。

10

Though he holds in his arms the earth-bride,
the sky is ever immensely away.

天空将大地新娘拥入怀里，
却始终与她隔着遥远的距离。

11

White and pink oleanders meet
and make merry in different dialects.

白白粉粉的夹竹桃相遇在一起,
用各自不同的方言说笑打闹着。

12

The freedom of the storm and the bondage of the stem
join hands in the dance of swaying branches.

风暴的放纵与树干的束缚
携手造就了枝杈的舞动飘摇。

13

Thou hast[1] vanished from my reach
leaving an impalpable touch in the blue of the sky,
an invisible image in the wind moving
among the shadows.

热词天地

1.hast [hæst] aux. 古英语中 have 的第二人称单数一般现在时

你从我指尖消失，
在蔚蓝的天空里留下无可察觉的触摸，
以及游弋在暗影之间的
一个看不见的风中影像。

14

My offerings are not for the temple
at the end of the road,
but for the wayside shrines
that surprise me at every bend.

我的奉献不是为了道路尽头的
赫赫神殿，
而是为了途中每个转弯处
那些不期而遇的小小神龛。

15

To carry the burden of the instrument,
count the cost of its material,
and never to know that it is for music,
is the tragedy of deaf life.

聋聩人生的悲剧在于
背负着沉重的乐器，
计算着它材料的成本，
却始终不知，它是为音乐而生的。

16

The blue of the sky longs for the earth's green,
the wind between them sighs, "Alas."
Day's pain muffled[1] by its own glare,
burns among stars in the night.

热词天地

1.muffled ['mʌfld] *adj.* 被隔的；听不清的；蒙住的

苍穹的蔚蓝渴望大地的绿色，
"唉，"微风在天地之间叹息。
白昼的痛苦被自身的强光掩盖，
夜晚却在繁星之间燃烧起来。

园丁集 （冰心译）

My Paper Boat

I remember a day in my childhood I floated a paper boat in the ditch.
It was a wet day of July; I was alone and happy over my play.
I floated my paper boat in the ditch.

Suddenly the storm clouds thickened[1], winds came in gusts, and rain poured in torrents[2].
Rills of muddy water rushed and swelled[3] the stream and sunk my boat.

Bitterly I thought in my mind that the storm came on purpose to spoil my happiness; all its malice was against me.

The cloudy day of July is long today, and I have been musing over all those games in life wherein I was loser.

I was blaming my fate for the many tricks it played on me, when suddenly I remembered the paper boat that sank in the ditch.

热词天地

1. thicken ['θɪkən] *v.* （使）变厚
2. torrent ['tɒrənt] *n.* 激流，奔流
3. swell [swel] *v.* 膨胀；隆起；增大
   on purpose 有目的地；故意地
   (be) against 反对；违背，不顾

我的纸船

我记得在童年时代,有一天,我在水沟里漂一只纸船。

那是七月的一个阴湿的天,我独自快乐地嬉戏。

我在沟里漂一只纸船。

忽然间阴云密布,狂风怒号,大雨倾注。

浑水像小河般流溢,把我的纸船冲没了。

我心里难过地想:这风暴是故意来破坏我的快乐的,它的一切恶意都是对着我的。

今天,七月的阴天是漫长的,我在默忆我生命中以我为失败者的一切游戏。

我抱怨命运,因为它屡次戏弄了我,当我忽然忆起我的沉在沟里的纸船的时候。

The Fair Before the Temple

The fair was on before the temple. It had rained from the early morning and the day came to its end.

Brighter than all the gladness of the crowd was the bright smile of a girl who bought for a farthing[1] a whistle of palm leaf.

The shrill joy of that whistle floated above all laughter and noise.

An endless throng of people came and jostled together. The road was muddy, the river in flood, the field under water in ceaseless[2] rain.

Greater than all the troubles of the crowd was a little boy's trouble—he had not a farthing to buy a painted stick.

His wistful[3] eyes gazing at the shop made this whole meeting of men so pitiful.

热词天地

1.farthing ['fɑːðɪŋ] *n.* 一点儿，极少量
2.ceaseless ['siːsləs] *adj.* 不断的；不停的
3.wistful ['wɪstfl] *adj.* 渴望的；沉思的，不满足似的
   the fair 老街上的市集
   gazing at 盯住；凝视

庙前的集会

庙前的集会正在进行。从一早起就下雨,这一天快过尽了。

比一切群众的欢乐还光辉的,是一个花一分钱买到一个棕叶哨子的小女孩的光辉的微笑。

哨子的尖脆欢乐的声音,在一切笑语喧哗之上飘浮。

无尽的人流挤在一起,路上泥泞,河水在涨,雨在不停地下着,田地都没在水里。

比一切群众的烦恼更深的,是一个小男孩的烦恼——他连买那根带颜色的小棍的一文钱都没有。

他苦闷的眼睛望着那间小店,使得这整个人类的集会变成可悲悯的。

The Workman's Little Daughter

The workman and his wife from the west country are busy digging to make bricks for the kiln.

Their little daughter goes to the landing-place[1] by the river; there she has no end of scouring and scrubbing of pots and pans.

Her little brother, with shaven head and brown, naked, mud-covered limbs, follows after her and waits patiently on the high bank at her bidding[2].

She goes back home with the full pitcher poised[3] on her head, the shining brass pot in her left hand, holding the child with her right—she the tiny servant of her mother, grave with the weight of the household cares.

One day I saw this naked boy sitting with legs outstretched.

In the water his sister sat rubbing a drinking-pot with a handful of earth, turning it round and round.

Near by a soft-haired lamb stood gazing along the bank.

It came close to where the boy sat and suddenly bleated aloud, and the child started up and screamed.

His sister left off cleaning her pot and ran up.

She took up her brother in one arm and the lamb in the other, and dividing her caresses between them bound in one bond of affection the offspring of beast and man.

热词天地

1.landing-place ['lændɪŋpleɪs] *n.* （飞机）着陆地，降落场；（船等）码头，靠岸处
2.bidding ['bɪdɪŋ] *n.* 投标；出价；命令   3.poised [pɔɪzd] *adj.* 镇定的；平衡的

工人的小女儿

西乡来的工人和他的妻子正忙着替砖窑挖土。

他们的小女儿到河边的渡头上;她无休无歇地擦洗锅盘。

她的小弟弟,光着头,赤裸着黧黑的涂满泥土的身躯,跟着她,听她的话,在高高的河岸上耐心地等着她。

她顶着满瓶的水,平稳地走回家中,左手提着发亮的铜壶,右手拉着那个孩子。——她是妈妈的小丫头,繁重的家务使她变得严肃了。

有一天我看见那赤裸的孩子伸着腿坐着。

他姐姐坐在水里,用一把土在转来转去地擦洗一把水壶。

附近站着一只毛茸茸的小羊羔,正凝视着河岸远方。

它走近这孩子身边,忽然大叫了一声,孩子吓得哭喊起来。

他姐姐放下水壶跑上岸来。

她一只手抱起弟弟,一只手抱起小羊,把她的爱抚分成两半;人类和动物的后代在慈爱的连结中合一了。

In May

It was in May. The sultry[1] noon seemed endlessly long. The dry earth gaped with thirst in the heat.

When I heard from the riverside a voice calling, "Come, my darling!"

I shut my book and opened the window to look out.

I saw a big buffalo[2] with mud-stained hide, standing near the river with placid, patient eyes; and a youth, knee deep in water, calling it to its bath.

I smiled amused[3] and felt a touch of sweetness in my heart.

热词天地

1. sultry ['sʌltrɪ] *adj.* 闷热的；狂暴的
2. buffalo ['bʌfələʊ] *n.* 水牛；野牛
3. amused [ə'mjuːzd] *adj.* 愉快的，顽皮的；被逗乐的

在五月天里

在五月天里，闷热的正午仿佛无尽地悠长。干地在灼热中渴的张着口。
当我听到河边有个声音叫道："来吧，我的宝贝！"
我合上书开窗外视。
我看见一只皮毛上尽是泥土的大水牛，眼光沉着地站在河边；
一个小伙子站在没膝的水中，在叫它去洗澡。
我高兴而微笑了，心里感到一阵甜柔的触动。

Listening

"Ah, poet, the evening draws near; your hair is turning grey."

"Do you in your lonely musing hear the message of the hereafter?"

"It is evening," the poet said," and I am listening because some one may call from the village, late though it be.

"I watch if young straying hearts meet together, and two pairs of eager eyes beg for music to break their silence and speak for them.

"Who is there to weave their passionate songs, if I sit on the shore of life and contemplate death and the beyond?

"The early evening star disappears.

"The glow of a funeral pyre slowly dies by the silent river.

"Jackals cry in chorus from the courtyard of the deserted house in the light of the worn-out moon.

"If some wanderer, leaving home, come here to watch the night and with bowed head listen to the murmur of the darkness, who is there to whisper the secrets of life into his ears if I shutting my doors, should try to free myself from mortal bonds?

"It is a trifle that my hair is turning grey.

"I am ever as young or as old as the youngest and the oldest of this village.

"Some have tears that well up in the daylight, and others tears that are hidden in the gloom.

"They all have need for me, and I have no time to brood over the afterlife.

"I am of an age with each, what matter if my hair turns grey?"

静听

"呵,诗人,夜晚渐临;你的头发已经变白。"

"在你孤寂的沉思中听到了来生的消息么?"

"是夜晚了。"诗人说,"夜虽已晚,我还在静听,因为也许有人会从村中呼唤。

"我看守着,是否有年轻的飘游的心聚在一起,两对渴望的眼睛切盼有音乐来打破他们的沉默,并替他们说话。

"如果我坐在生命的岸边默想着死亡和来世,又有谁来编写他们的热情的诗歌呢?

"早现的晚星消隐了。

"火葬灰中的红光在沉静的河边慢慢地熄灭下去。

"残月的微光下,胡狼从空宅的庭院里齐声嗥叫。

"假如有游子们离了家,到这里来守夜,低头静听黑暗的微语,有谁把生命的秘密向他耳边低诉呢,如果我关起门户,企图摆脱世俗的牵缠?

"我的头发变白是一件小事。

"我是永远和这村里最年轻的人一样的年轻,最年老的人一样的年老。

"有的人发出甜柔单纯的微笑,有的人眼里含着狡狯的闪光。

"有的人在白天流涌着眼泪,有的人的眼泪却隐藏在幽暗里。

"他们都需要我,我没有时间去冥想来生。

"我和每一个人都是同年的,我的头发变白了又该怎样呢?"

Gifts

In the morning I cast my net into the sea.

I dragged up from the dark abyss things of strange aspect and strange beauty—some shone like a smile, some glistened like tears, and some were flushed like the cheeks of a bride.

When with the day's burden I went home, my love was sitting in the garden idly tearing the leaves of a flower.

I hesitated for a moment, and then placed at her feet all that I had dragged up, and stood silent.

She glanced at them and said, "What strange things are these, I know not of what use they are!"

I bowed my head in shame and thought, "I have not fought for these, I did not buy them in the market; they are not fit gifts for her."

Then the whole night through I flung them one by one into the street.

In the morning travellers came; they picked them up and carried them into far countries.

礼物

早晨我把网撒在海里。

我从沉黑的深渊拉出奇形奇美的东西——有些微笑般地发亮,有些眼泪般地闪光,有的晕红得像新娘的双颊。

当我携带着这一天的担负回到家里的时候,我爱人正坐在园里悠闲地扯着花叶。

我沉吟了一会,就把我捞得的一切放在她的脚前,沉默地站着。

她瞥了一眼说:"这是些什么怪东西?我不知道这些东西有什么用处!"我羞愧得低了头,心想:"我并没有为这些东西去奋斗,也不是从市场里买来的;这不是一些配送给她的礼物。"

整夜的工夫我把这些东西一件一件地丢到街上。

早晨行路的人来了;他们把这些拾起带到远方去了。

 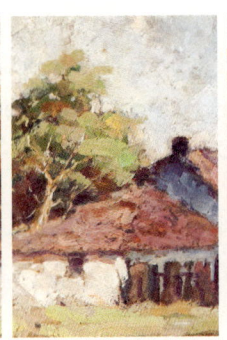 

Turn Them Away I Cannot

Ah me, why did they build my house by the road to the market town?
They moor their laden boats near my trees.
They come and go and wander at their will.
I sit and watch them; my time wears on.

Turn them away I cannot. And thus my days pass by.
Night and day their steps sound by my door.
Vainly I cry, "I do not know you."
Some of them are known to my fingers, some to my nostrils, the blood in my veins seems to know them, and some are known to my dreams.
Turn them away I cannot. I call them and say, "Come to my house whoever chooses. Yes, come."

In the morning the bell rings in the temple.
They came with baskets in their hands.
Their feet are rosy-red. The early light of dawn is on their faces.
Turn them away I cannot. I call them and I say, "Come to my garden to gather flowers. Come hither."

In the mid-day the gong sounds at the palace gate.
I know not why they leave their work and linger near my hedge.

The flowers in their hair are pale and faded; the notes are languid in their flutes.

Turn them away I cannot. I call them and say, "The shade is cool under my trees. Come, friends."

At night the crickets chirp in the woods.

Who is it that comes slowly to my door and gently knocks?

I vaguely see the face, not a word is spoken, the stillness of the sky is all around.

Turn away my silent guest I cannot. I look at the face through the dark, and hours of dreams pass by.

我不能回绝他们

我真烦,为什么他们把我的房子盖在通向市镇的路边呢?
他们把满载的船只拴在我的树上。
他们任意地来去游逛。
我坐着看着他们;光阴都消磨了。

我不能回绝他们。这样我的日子便过去了。
日日夜夜他们的足音在我门前震荡。
我徒然地叫道,"我不认识你们。"
有些人是我的手指所认识的,有些人是我的鼻官所认识的,我脉管中的血液似乎认得他们,有些人是我的魂梦所认识的。
我不能回绝他们。我呼唤他们说,"谁愿意到我房子里来就请来吧。对了,来吧。"

清晨庙里的钟声敲起。

他们提着筐子来了。

他们的脚像玫瑰般红。熹微的晨光照在他们的脸上。

我不能回绝他们。我呼唤他们说,"到我园里来采花吧。到这里来吧。"

中午锣声在庙殿门前敲起。

我不知道他们为什么放下工作在我篱畔流连。

他们发上的花朵已经褪色枯萎了,他们横笛里的音调也显得乏倦。

我不能回绝他们。我呼唤他们说,"我的树荫下是凉爽的。来吧,朋友们。"

夜里蟋蟀在林中唧唧地叫。

是谁慢慢地来到我的门前轻轻地敲叩?

我模糊地看到他的脸,他一句话也没说,四周是天空的静默。

我不能回绝我的沉默的客人。我从黑暗中望着他的脸,梦幻的时间过去了。

The Young Prince Is to Pass by Our Door

O mother, the young Prince is to pass by our door,—how can I attend to my work this morning?
Show me how to braid up my hair; tell me what garment to put on.
Why do you look at me amazed, mother?

I know well he will not glance up once at my window; I know he will pass out of my sight in the twinkling of an eye; only the vanishing strain of the flute will come sobbing to me from afar.
But the young Prince will pass by our door, and I will put on my best for the moment.

O mother, the young Prince did pass by our door, and the morning sun flashed from his chariot.
I swept aside the veil from my face, I tore the ruby chain from my neck and flung it in his path.
Why do you look at me amazed, mother?

I know well he did not pick up my chain; I know it was crushed under his wheels leaving a red stain upon the dust, and no one knows what my gift was nor to whom.
But the young Prince did pass by our door, and I flung the jewel from my breast before his path.

年轻的王子要从我们门前走过

啊,母亲,年轻的王子要从我们门前走过,——今天早晨我哪有心思干活呢?

教给我怎样挽发;告诉我应该穿哪件衣裳。

你为什么惊讶地望着我呢,母亲?

我深知他不会仰视我的窗户;我知道一刹那间他就要走出我的视线以外;只有那残曳的笛声将从远处向我呜咽。

但是那年轻的王子将从我们门前走过,这时节我要穿上我最好的衣裳。

啊,母亲,年轻的王子已经从我们门前走过了,从他的车辇里射出朝日的金光。

我从脸上掠开面纱,我从颈上扯下红玉的颈环,扔在他走来的路上。

你为什么惊讶地望着我呢,母亲?

我深知他没有拾起我的颈环;我知道它在他的轮下碾碎了,在尘土上留下了红斑,没有人晓得我的礼物是什么样子,也不知道是给谁的。

但是那年轻的王子曾经从我们门前走过,我也曾经把我胸前的珍宝丢在他走来的路上了。

She Is I

When the lamp went out by my bed I woke up with the early birds.

I sat at my open window with a fresh wreath on my loose hair.

The young traveller came along the road in the rosy mist of the morning.

A pearl chain was on his neck, and the sun's ray fell on his crown. He stopped before my door and asked me with an eager cry, "Where is she?"

For very shame I could not say, "She is I, young traveller, she is I."

It was dusk and the lamp was not lit.

I was listlessly braiding my hair.

The young traveller came on his chariot in the glow of the setting sun.

His horses were foaming at the mouth, and there was dust on his gament.

He alighted at my door and asked in a tired voice, "Where is she?"

For very shame I could not say, "She is I, weary traveller, she is I."

It is an April night. The lamp is burning in my room.

The breeze of the south comes gently. The noisy parrot sleeps in its cage.

My bodice is the colour of the peacock's throat, and my mantle is green as young grass.

I sit upon the floor at the window watching the deserted street.

Through the dark night I keep humming, "She is I, despairing traveller, she is I."

她就是我

当我床前的灯熄灭了,我和晨鸟一同醒起。
我在散发上戴上新鲜的花串,坐在洞开的窗前。
那年轻的行人在玫瑰色的朝霭中从大路上来了。

珠链在他的颈上,阳光在他的冠上。他停在我的门前,用切望的呼声问我:"她在哪里呢?"
因为深深害羞,我不好意思说出:"她就是我,年轻的行人,她就是我。"

黄昏来到,还未上灯。
我心绪不宁地编着头发。
在落日的光辉中年轻的行人驾着车辇来了。
他的驾车的马,嘴里喷着白沫,他的衣袍上蒙着尘土。

他在我的门前下车,用疲乏的声音问:"她在哪里呢?"
因为深深害羞,我不好意思说出:"她就是我,愁倦的行人,她就是我。"

一个四月的夜晚。我的屋里点着灯。
南风温柔地吹来。多言的鹦鹉在笼里睡着了。
我的衷衣和孔雀颈毛一样地华彩,我的披纱和嫩草一样地碧青。
我坐在窗前地上看望着冷落的街道。
在沉黑的夜中我不住地低吟着,"她就是我,失望的行人,她就是我。"

When I Go alone to My Love-Tryst

When I go alone at night to my love-tryst, birds do not sing, the wind does not stir, the houses on both sides of the street stand silent.

It is my own anklets that grow loud at every step and I am ashamed.

When I sit on my balcony and listen for his footsteps, leaves do not rustle on the trees, and the water is still in the river like the sword on the knees of a sentry fallen asleep.

It is my own heart that beats wildly—I do not know how to quiet it.

When my love comes and sits by my side, when my body trembles and my eyelids droop, the night darkens, the wind blows out the lamp, and the clouds draw veils over the stars.

It is the jewel at my own breast that shines and gives light. I do not know how to hide it.

当我独赴幽会的时候

当我在夜里独赴幽会的时候,鸟儿不叫,风儿不吹,街道两旁的房屋沉默地站立着。

是我自己的脚镯越走越响,使我感到羞怯。

当我站在凉台上倾听他的足音,树叶不摇,河水静止像熟睡的哨兵膝上的刀剑。

是我自己的心在狂跳——我不知道怎样使它宁静。

当我爱来了,坐在我身旁,当我的身躯震颤,我的眼睫下垂,夜更深了,风吹灯灭,云片在繁星上曳过轻纱。

是我自己胸前的珍宝放出光明。我不知道怎样把它遮起。

Let Your Work Be! Bride

Let your work be, bride. Listen, the guest has come.

Do you hear, he is gently shaking the chain which fastens the door?

See that your anklets make no loud noise, and that your step is not overhurried at meeting him.

Let your work be, bride, the guest has come in the evening.

No, it is not the ghostly wind, bride, do not be frightened.

It is the full moon on a night of April; shadows are pale in the courtyard; the sky overhead is bright.

Draw your veil over your face if you must; carry the lamp to the door if you fear.

No, it is not the ghostly wind, bride, do not be frightened.

Have no word with him if you are shy; stand aside by the door when you meet him.

If he asks you questions, and if you wish to, you can lower your eyes in silence.

Do not let your bracelets jingle when, lamp in hand, you lead him in.

Have no word with him if you are shy.

Have you not finished your work yet, bride? Listen, the guest has come.

Have you not lit the lamp in the cowshed?

Have you not got ready the offering basket for the evening service?

Have you not put the red lucky mark at the parting of your hair, and done your toilet for the night?

O bride, do you hear, the guest has come?

Let your work be!

放下你的工作吧，我的新娘

放下你的工作吧，我的新娘。听，客人来了。
你听见没有，他在轻轻地摇动那拴门的链子？
小心不要让你的脚镯响出声音，在迎接他的时候你的脚步不要太急。
放下你的工作吧，新娘，客人在晚上来了。
不，这不是一阵阴风，新娘，不要惊惶。
这是四月夜中的满月，院里的影子是暗淡的，头上的天空是明亮的。
把轻纱遮上脸，若是你觉得需要；提着灯到门前去，若是你害怕。
不，这不是一阵阴风，新娘，不要惊惶。
若是你害羞就不必和他说话，你迎接他的时候只须站在门边。
他若问你话，若是你愿意这样做，你就沉默地低眸。
不要让你的手镯作响，当你提着灯，带他进来的时候。
不必同他说话，如果你害羞。

你的工作还没有做完么，新娘？听，客人来了。
你还没有把牛栅里的灯点起来么？
你还没有把晚祷的供筐准备好么？
你还没有在发缝中涂上鲜红的吉祥点，你还没有理过晚妆么？
啊，新娘，你没有听见，客人来了么？
放下你的工作吧！

Come as You Are

Come as you are; do not loiter over your toilet.

If your braided hair has loosened, if the parting of your hair be not straight, if the ribbons of your bodice be not fastened, do not mind.

Come as you are; do not loiter over your toilet.
Come, with quick steps over the grass.

If the raddle come from your feet because of the dew, if the rings of bells upon your feet slacken, if pearls drop out of your chain, do not mind.

Come with quick steps over the grass.
Do you see the clouds wrapping the sky?

Flocks of cranes fly up from the further river-bank and fitful guests of wind rush over the heath.

The anxious cattle run to their stalls in the village.

Do you see the clouds wrapping the sky?

In vain you light your toilet lamp—it flickers and goes out in the wind.

Who can know that your eyelids have not been touched with lampblack? For your eyes are darker than rain-clouds.

In vain you light your toilet lamp—it goes out.

Come as you are; do not loiter over your toilet.

If the wreath is not woven, who cares; if the wrist-chain has not been linked, let it be.

The sky is overcast with clouds—it is late.

Come as you are; do not loiter over your toilet.

你就这样地来吧

你就这样地来吧;不要在梳妆上挨延了。

即使你的辫发松散,即使你的发缝没有分直,即使你衷衣的丝带没有系好,都不要管它。

你就这样地来吧;不要在梳妆上挨延了。
来吧,用快步踏过草坪。

即使露水沾掉了你脚上的红粉,即使你踝上的铃串褪松,即使你链上的珠儿脱落,都不要管它。

来吧,用快步踏过草坪。
你没看见云雾遮住天空么?
鹤群从远远的河岸飞起,狂风吹过常青的灌木。
惊牛奔向村里的栅棚。
你没看见云雾遮住天空么?

你徒然点上晚妆的灯火——它颤摇着在风中熄灭了。
谁能看出你眼睫上没有涂上乌烟?因为你的眼睛比雨云还黑。
你徒然点上晚妆的灯火——它熄灭了。

你就这样地来吧,不要在梳妆上挨延了。
即使花环没有穿好,谁管它呢;即使手镯没有扣上,让它去吧。
天空被阴云塞满了——时间已晚。

你就这样地来吧;不要在梳妆上挨延了。

Come to My Lake

If you would be busy and fill your pitcher, come, O come to my lake.

The water will cling round your feet and babble its secret.

The shadow of the coming rain is on the sands, and the clouds hang low upon the blue lines of the trees like the heavy hair above your eyebrows.

I know well the rhythm of your steps, they are beating in my heart.

Come, O come to my lake, if you must fill your pitcher.

If you would be idle and sit listless and let your pitcher float on the water, come, O come to my lake.

The grassy slope is green, and the wild flowers beyond number.

Your thoughts will stray out of your dark eyes like birds from their nests.

Your veil will drop to your feet.

Come, O come to my lake if you must sit idle.
If you would leave off your play and dive in the water, come, O come to my lake.
Let your blue mantle lie on the shore; the blue water will cover you and hide you.
The waves will stand a-tiptoe to kiss your neck and whisper in your ears.

Come, O come to my lake, if you would dive in the water.
If you must be mad and leap to your death, come, O come to my lake.
It is cool and fathomlessly deep.
It is dark like a sleep that is dreamless.
There in its depths nights and days are one, and songs are silence.

Come, O come to my lake, if you would plunge to your death.

到我的湖上来吧

若是你要忙着把水瓶灌满,来吧,到我的湖上来吧。
湖水将回绕在你的脚边,潺潺地说出它的秘密。
沙滩上有了欲来的雨云的阴影,云雾低垂在丛树的绿线上,像你眉上的浓发。
我深深地熟悉你脚步的韵律,它在我心中敲击。

来吧,到我的湖上来吧,如果你必须把水瓶灌满。
如果你想懒散闲坐,让你的水瓶飘浮在水面,来吧,到我的湖上来吧。
草坡碧绿,野花多得数不清。
你的思想将从你乌黑的眼眸中飞出,像鸟儿飞出窝巢。
你的披纱将褪落到脚上。

来吧,如果你要闲坐,到我的湖上来吧。
如果你想撇下嬉游跳进水里,来吧,到我的湖上来吧。
把你的蔚蓝的丝布留在岸上;蔚蓝的水将没过你,盖住你。
水波将蹑足来吻你的颈项,在你耳边低语。

来吧,如果你想跳进水里,到我的湖上来吧。
如果你想发狂而投入死亡,来吧,到我的湖上来吧。
它是清凉的,深到无底。
它沉黑得像无梦的睡眠。
在它的深处黑夜就是白天,歌曲就是静默。

来吧,如果你想投入死亡,到我的湖上来吧。

I Did Not Come near You

I asked nothing, only stood at the edge of the wood behind the tree.
Languor was still upon the eyes of the dawn, and the dew in the air.

The lazy smell of the damp grass hung in the thin mist above the earth.

Under the banyan tree you were milking the cow with your hands, tender and fresh as butter.

And I was standing still.

I did not say a word. It was the bird that sang unseen from the thicket.

The mango tree was shedding its flowers upon the village road, and the bees came humming one by one.

On the side of the pond the gate of Shiva's temple was open and the worshipper had begun his chants.

With the vessel on your lap you were milking the cow.

I stood with my empty can.

I did not come near you.

The sky woke with the sound of the gong at the temple.

The dust was raised in the road from the hoofs of the driven cattle.

With the gurgling pitchers at their hips, women came from the river.

Your bracelets were jingling, and foam brimming over the jar.

The morning wore on and I did not come near you.

我没有走近你

我一无所求,只站在林边树后。
倦意还逗留在黎明的眼上,露润在空气里。
湿草的懒味悬垂在地面的薄雾中。
在榕树下你用乳油般柔嫩的手挤着牛奶。

我沉静地站立着。
我没有说出一个字。那是藏起的鸟儿在密叶中歌唱。
芒果树在乡间的小路上撒着繁花,蜜蜂一只一只地嗡嗡飞来。
池塘边湿婆天的庙门开了,朝拜者开始诵经。
你把罐儿放在膝上挤着牛奶。
我提着空桶站立着。
我没有走近你。

天空和庙里的锣声一同醒起。
街尘在驱走的牛蹄下飞扬。
把汩汩发响的水瓶搂在腰上,女人们从河边走来。
你的钏镯丁当,乳沫溢出罐沿。
晨光渐逝而我没有走近你。

吉檀迦利 （冰心 译）

Seashore

On the seashore of endless worlds children meet. The infinite sky is motionless[1] overhead and the restless water is boisterous. On the seashore of endless worlds the children meet with shouts and dances.

They build their houses with sand and they play with empty shells. With withered[2] leaves they weave their boats and smilingly float them on the vast deep. Children have their play on the seashore of worlds.

They know not how to swim, they know not how to cast nets. Pearl fishers dive for pearls, merchants sail in their ships, while children gather pebbles and scatter them again. They seek not for hidden treasures, they know not how to cast nets.

The sea surges up with laughter, and pale gleams the smile of the sea beach.

热词天地

1.motionless ['məʊʃnləs] *adj.* 静止的   2.withered ['wɪðəd] *adj.* 枯萎的

海滨

　　孩子们在无边的世界的海滨聚会。头上是静止的无垠的天空,不宁的海波奔腾喧闹。在无边的世界的海滨,孩子们欢呼跳跃地聚会着。

　　他们用沙子盖起房屋,用空贝壳来游戏。他们把枯叶编成小船,微笑着把它们漂浮在深远的海上。孩子在世界的海滨做着游戏。

　　他们不会凫水,他们也不会撒网。采珠的人潜水寻珠,商人们奔波航行,孩子们收集了石子却又把它们丢弃了。他们不搜求宝藏,他们也不会撒网。

　　大海涌起了喧笑,海岸闪烁着苍白的微笑。

Colored Toys

When I bring to you coloured toys, my child, I understand why there is such a play of colours on clouds, on water, and why flowers are painted in tints[1] — when I give coloured toys to you, my child.

When I sing to make you dance I truly know why there is music in leaves, and why waves send their chorus[2] of voices to the heart of the listening earth—when I sing to make you dance.

When I bring sweet things to your greedy[3] hands I know why there is honey in the cup of the flowers and why fruits are secretly filled with sweet juice—when I bring sweet things to your greedy hands.

When I kiss your face to make you smile, my darling, I surely understand what pleasure streams from the sky in morning light, and what delight that is which the summer breeze brings to my body—when I kiss you to make you smile.

热词天地

1. tint [tɪnt] *n.* 色彩 *v.* 染色；着色于……
2. chorus ['kɔːrəs] *n.* 合唱队；齐声；歌舞队 *vt.* 合唱；异口同声地说
3. greedy ['griːdɪ] *adj.* 贪婪的；贪吃的；渴望的
   summer breeze 夏日微风

彩色玩具

当我送你彩色玩具的时候,我的孩子,我了解为什么云中水上会幻弄出这许多颜色,为什么花朵都用颜色染起——当我送你彩色玩具的时候,我的孩子。

当我唱歌使你跳舞的时候,我彻底地知道为什么树叶上响出音乐,为什么波浪把它们的合唱送进静听的大地的心头——当我唱歌使你跳舞的时候。

当我把糖果递到你贪婪的手中的时候,我懂得为什么花心里有蜜,为什么水果里隐藏着甜汁——当我把糖果递到你贪婪的手中的时候。

当我吻你的脸使你微笑的时候,我的宝贝,我的确了解晨光从天空流下时,是怎样得高兴,暑天的凉风吹到我身上的是怎样得愉快——当我吻你的脸使你微笑的时候。

新月集

The Sourec

The sleep that flits on baby's eyes—does anybody know from where it comes? Yes, there is a rumour that it has its dwelling where, in the fairy village among shadows of the forest dimly lit with glow-worms, there hang two shy buds of enchantment[1]. From there it comes to kiss baby's eyes.

The smile that flickers[2] on baby's lips when he sleeps—does anybody know where it was born? Yes, there is a rumour that a young pale beam of a crescent moon touched the edge of a vanishing[3] autumn cloud, and there the smile was first born in the dream of a dew-washed morning—the smile that flickers on baby's lips when he sleeps.

The sweet, soft freshness that blooms on baby's limbs—does anybody know where it was hidden so long? Yes, when the mother was a young girl it lay pervading[4] her heart in tender and silent mystery of love—the sweet, soft freshness that has bloomed on baby's limbs.

热词天地

1.enchantment [ɪnˈtʃɑːntmənt] n. 魅力；魔法　　2.flicker [ˈflɪkə] vi. 闪烁；颤动
3.vanishing [ˈvænɪʃ] adj. 消没的　　4.pervade [pəˈveɪd] vt. 遍及

来源

　　这掠过婴儿眼上的睡眠——有谁知道它是从哪里来的吗？是的，有谣传说它住在林荫中萤火朦胧照着的仙村里，那里挂着两只甜柔迷人的花蕾。它从那里来吻着婴儿的眼睛。

　　婴儿睡梦中唇上闪现的微笑——有谁知道它是从哪里生出来的吗？是的，有谣传说这是一线新月的微笑触到了消散的秋云的边缘，微笑就在被朝雾洗净的晨梦中，第一次生出来了——这就是那婴儿睡梦中唇上闪现的微笑。

　　在婴儿的四肢上，散发着花朵般的甜柔清新的生气，有谁知道它是在哪里藏了这么许久吗？是的，当母亲还是一个少女时，它就在温柔安静的爱的神秘中，充塞在她的心里了——这就是那婴儿四肢上散发的甜柔新鲜的生气。

The Land Of The Exile

Mother, the light has grown grey in the sky; I do not know what the time is.

There is no fun in my play, so I have come to you. It is Saturday, our holiday.

Leave off your work, mother; sit here by the window and tell me where the desert of Tepântar in the fairy tale is?

The shadow of the rains has covered the day from end to end.

The fierce[1] lightning is scratching the sky with its nails.

When the clouds rumble and it thunders, I love to be afraid in my heart and cling to you.

When the heavy rain patters for hours on the bamboo leaves, and our windows shake and rattle at the gusts[2] of wind, I like to sit alone in the room, mother, with you, and hear you talk about the desert of Tepântar in the fairy tale.

Where is it, mother, on the shore of what sea, at the foot of what hills, in the kingdom of what king?

There are no hedges there to mark the fields, no footpath across it

by which the villagers reach their village in the evening, or the woman who gathers dry sticks in the forest can bring her load to the market. With patches of yellow grass in the sand and only one tree where the pair of wise old birds have their nest, lies the desert of Tepântar.

I can imagine how, on just such a cloudy day, the young son of the king is riding alone on a grey horse through the desert, in search of the princess who lies imprisoned in the giant's palace across that unknown water.

When the haze of the rain comes down in the distant sky, and lightning starts up like a sudden fit of pain, does he remember his unhappy mother, abandoned by the king, sweeping the cow-stall and wiping her eyes, while he rides through the desert of Tepântar in the fairy tale?

See, mother, it is almost dark before the day is over, and there are no travellers yonder[3] on the village road.

The shepherd boy has gone home early from the pasture, and men have left their fields to sit on mats under the eaves of their huts, watching the scowling[4] clouds.

Mother, I have left all my books on the shelf—do not ask me to do my lessons now.

When I grow up and am big like my father, I shall learn all that must be learnt.

But just for to-day, tell me, mother, where the desert of Tepântar in the fairy tale is?

热词天地

1. fierce [fɪəs] *adj.* 凶猛的；猛烈的；暴躁的
2. gust [gʌst] *n.* 风味；一阵狂风；趣味 *vi.* 一阵阵地劲吹
3. yonder ['jɒndə] *adj.* 那边的，远处的 *adv.* 在那边；在远处
4. scowling [skaulɪŋ] *adj.* 愁眉不展的；闷闷不乐的

   leave off 停止   cling to 坚持；依靠；依附；紧握不放

流放之地

妈妈,天空中的光成了灰色;我不知道是什么时间了。

我玩得很没趣,所以到你这儿来。今天是星期六,我们的假日。

放下你手中的活,妈妈;坐在窗边,告诉我童话里的特潘塔沙漠在什么地方?

雨的影子遮天蔽日。

凶猛的闪电用利爪划破长空。

当乌云翻滚,电闪雷鸣,我乐于心怀恐惧地趴到你身上。

当大雨倾泻在竹叶上许久,我们的窗子被狂风震动,我就爱独自和你坐在屋里,妈妈,听你讲童话里特潘塔沙漠的故事。

它在哪儿,妈妈,在哪片海洋的岸上,在哪些山峰的脚下,在哪个国王的国土里?

田里没有此疆彼壤的界石，也没有村人日落归家时，或妇人在林间捡拾枯枝带到市场上去时，踩出的路。沙地上只有小块的黄草地和一棵树，一对聪明的老鸟儿在那里建了窝，那儿就是特潘塔沙漠吗？

　　我能想象到，在这样一个阴云漫布的日子，国王年轻的儿子，怎样地独自骑着一匹灰马，走过这沙漠，去寻那被囚禁在未知的重洋之外的巨人宫中的公主。

　　当雨雾自天际降落，闪电像突发的痛苦般袭来，当他骑马走过童话里的特潘塔沙漠的时候，他可记得他不幸的母亲，已为国王所弃，正在打扫牛棚，眼里流着眼泪？

　　看，妈妈，一天还没有完，天色已快黑了，那边村庄的道路上也没了旅客。

　　牧童早早从牧场上归家，人们都已从田里回来，坐在草屋檐下的草席上，望着阴霾的云层。

　　妈妈，我把我所有的书本都放在书架上了——不要让我现在做功课。

　　当我长大，大得像爸爸一样时，我将学到那必须学会的东西。

　　但是今天，你可得告诉我，妈妈，童话里的特潘塔沙漠在什么地方？

第一卷　仙人世界

Fairyland

If people came to know where my king's palace is, it would vanish[1] into the air.

The walls are of white silver and the roof of shining gold.

The queen lives in a palace with seven courtyards, and she wears a jewel that cost all the wealth of seven kingdoms.

But let me tell you, mother, in a whisper, where my king's palace is.

It is at the corner of our terrace[2] where the pot of the tulsi plant stands.

The princess lies sleeping on the far-away shore of the seven impassable[3] seas.

There is none in the world who can find her but myself.

She has bracelets on her arms and pearl drops in her ears; her hair sweeps down upon the floor.

She will wake when I touch her with my magic wand, and jewels will fall from her lips when she smiles.

But let me whisper in your ear, mother; she is there in the corner of our terrace where the pot of the tulsi plant stands.

When it is time for you to go to the river for your bath, step up to that terrace on the roof.

I sit in the corner where the shadows of the walls meet together.

Only puss is allowed to come with me, for she knows where the barber in the story lives.

But let me whisper, mother, in your ear where the barber in the story lives.

It is at the corner of the terrace where the pot of the tulsi plant stands.

热词天地

1. vanish ['vænɪʃ] *vi.* 消失；突然不见 *vt.* 使不见；使消失
2. terrace ['terəs] *n.* 平台；梯田；阳台
3. impassable [ɪm'pɑːsəb(ə)l] *adj.* 不能通行的；无路可通的

   in a whisper 低声地；悄声地
   magic wand 魔杖；魔术棒
   be allowed to 被允许做某事

仙境

如果人们知道了我的国王的宫殿在哪里,它就会消失在空气中。

墙壁是如雪的银,屋顶是耀眼的金。

皇后住在有七个庭院的宫苑里;她戴的一串珠宝,价值整整七个王国的全部财富。

不过,让我悄悄地告诉你,妈妈,我的国王的宫殿到底在哪里。

它就在我们阳台的角落,在那放着杜尔茜花花盆的地方。

公主在遥远的、七个无法逾越的重洋的对岸沉睡着。

除了我,世上便再没人能找到她。

她臂戴镯子,耳挂珍珠,长发及地。

当我用魔杖触碰她时,她便会醒来,而当她微笑时,珠玉将从她唇边滑落。

不过,让我在你耳边悄悄地告诉你吧,妈妈;她就住在我们阳台的角落,在那放着杜尔茜花花盆的地方。

当你要到河里洗澡的时候,你走上屋顶的那座阳台来罢。

我就坐在墙的阴影交会的一个角落里。

我只让小猫儿跟我在一起,因为它知道那故事里的理发匠住的地方。

不过,让我在你的耳边悄悄地告诉你,那故事里的理发匠到底住在哪里。

他住的地方,就在阳台的角上,在那放着杜尔茜花花盆的地方。

The Further Bank

I LONG to go over there to the further bank of the river,
Where those boats are tied to the bamboo poles in a line;
Where men cross over in their boats in the morning with ploughs on their shoulders[1] to till their far-away fields;
Where the cowherds make their lowing cattle swim across to the riverside pasture;
Whence they all come back home in the evening, leaving the jackals to howl in the island overgrown with weeds,
Mother, if you don't mind, I should like to become the boatman of the ferry when I am grown up.

They say there are strange pools hidden behind that high bank,
Where flocks of wild ducks come when the rains are over, and thick reeds grow round the margins where waterbirds lay their eggs;
Where snipes with their dancing tails stamp[2] their tiny footprints upon the clean soft mud;
Where in the evening the tall grasses crested with white flowers invite the moonbeam to float upon their waves.
Mother, if you don't mind, I should like to become the boatman of the ferryboat when I am grown up.

I shall cross and cross back from bank to bank, and all the boys and girls of the village will wonder at me while they are bathing.
When the sun climbs the mid sky and morning wears on to noon, I shall come running to you, saying, "Mother, I am hungry!"

When the day is done and the shadows cower under the trees, I shall come back in the dusk.

I shall never go away from you into the town to work like father.

Mother, if you don't mind, I should like to become the boatman of the ferryboat when I am grown up.

热词天地

1. shoulder [ˈʃəʊldə] *n.* 肩膀；肩部
2. stamp [stæmp] *n.* 邮票；印记；标志；跺脚 *vt.* 铭记；贴邮票于……；用脚踩踏

be tied to 束缚于，捆绑于
cross over 横渡；压步
wonder at 对……感到吃惊
wear on 缓慢地进行；时间消逝

远岸

我渴望到河的远岸去。

在那边,好些船只一行儿系在竹杆上;

人们在早晨乘船渡河,肩上扛着犁头,去耕耘他们的远处的田;

在那边,牧人使他们鸣叫着的牛游到河边的牧场去;

黄昏的时候,他们都回家了,只留下豺狼在这满长着野草的岛上哀叫。

妈妈,如果你不介意,我长大以后,要做这渡船的船夫。

据说有好些古怪的池塘藏在这个高岸背后。

在那里,下过雨,成群的野鸭飞至,茂盛的芦苇在岸边四围生长,水鸟在那里生蛋;

在那里,竹鸡带着舞动的尾巴,将它们细小的足迹印在洁净的软泥上;

在那里,夜晚,长草顶着白花,邀月光浮游在他们起伏的波浪上。

妈妈,如果你不介意,我长大以后,要做这渡船的船夫。

我要自此岸至彼岸,渡过来,渡过去,所有村中正在那儿沐浴的男孩女孩,都要诧异地望着我。

太阳升到中天,早晨变为正午了,我将跑到你那里去,说道:"妈妈,我饿了!"

一天完了,影子俯伏在树底下,我便要在黄昏中归家。

我将永不同爸爸那样,离开你到城里去做事。

妈妈,如果你不在意,我长大以后,要做这渡船的船夫。

The Champa Flower

Supposing[1] I became a champa flower, just for fun, and grew on a branch high up that tree, and shook in the wind with laughter and danced upon the newly budded[2] leaves, would you know me, mother?

You would call, "Baby, where are you?" and I should laugh to myself and keep quite quiet.

I should slyly[3] open my petals and watch you at your work.

When after your bath, with wet hair spread on your shoulders, you walked through the shadow of the champa tree to the little court where you say your prayers, you would notice the scent of the flower, but not know that it came from me.

When after the midday meal you sat at the window reading

Ramayana, and the tree's shadow fell over your hair and your lap, I should fling my wee little shadow on to the page of your book, just where you were reading.

But would you guess that it was the tiny shadow of your little child?

When in the evening you went to the cow-shed with the lighted lamp in your hand, I should suddenly drop on to the earth again and be your own baby once more, and beg you to tell me a story.

"Where have you been, you naughty child?"

"I won't tell you, mother." That's what you and I would say then.

热词天地

1. supposing [sə'pəʊzɪŋ] *conj.* 假如；不妨去……吧
2. budded ['bʌdɪd] *adj.* 有蓓蕾的；发了芽的
3. slyly [slaɪlɪ] *adv.* 狡猾地；秘密地；俏皮地

金色花

假如我变成了一朵金色花,只是为了嬉戏,长在那树的高枝上,笑哈哈地在风中摇曳,又在新生的树叶上跳舞,妈妈,你会认得我吗?

你要是叫道:"孩子,你在哪里呀?"我会暗自窃笑,却一声儿不吭。

我要悄悄地绽开花瓣儿,看着你工作。

当你沐浴后,湿发披肩,穿过金色花的树荫,走到你做祷告的小庭院时,你会嗅到这花儿的香气,却不知道这香气是自我而来。

当你吃过中饭,坐在窗前读《罗摩衍那》,那棵树的阴影落在你的头发与膝上时,我便要投我小小的影子在你的书页上,正投在你所读的地方。

但是你会猜得出这就是你孩子的小影子么?

当你傍晚拿着灯到牛棚去,我要突然落在地上,再次成为你的孩子,求你讲个故事给我听。

"你到哪里去了,你这淘气的孩子?"

"我不告诉你,妈妈。"这就是你我之间的对话。

第一卷 仙人世界 81

采果集

My life when young was like a flower—a flower that loosens a petal or two from her abundance[1] and never feels the loss when the spring breeze comes to beg at her door.

Now at the end of youth my life is like a fruit, having nothing to spare[2], and waiting to offer herself completely with her full burden[3] of sweetness.

热词天地

1. abundance [əˈbʌndəns] *n.* 充裕；丰富
2. spare [speə(r)] *vt.* 节约，吝惜；饶恕；分出，分让
3. burden [ˈbɜːdn] *n.* 负担；责任

　　我年轻时的生命如一朵花——当和煦的春风来到她门口乞求之时，她从充裕的花瓣中慷慨地解下一片两片，从未感觉到这是损失。

　　如今青春已逝，我的生命如同一颗果实，已无物可施，只等着彻底地奉献自己，连同那沉甸甸的甜蜜。

第二卷 莲花

飞鸟集

1

The great earth makes herself hospitable[1] with the help of the grass.

热词天地

1.hospitable [hɒ'spɪtəbl] *adj.* 热情友好的；（环境）舒适的

大地在绿茵的帮助下，
显出她自己的热情好客。

2

His own mornings are new surprises to God.

神自己的清晨,在他看来也是新奇的。

3

"How far are you from me, O Fruit?"
"I am hidden in your heart, O Flower."

"你离我有多远呢,果儿?"
"我就藏在你的心里啊,花儿。"

4

"The learned say that your lights will one day be no more," said the firefly[1] to the stars.
The stars made no answer.

热词天地

1. firefly ['faɪəflaɪ] *n.* [昆] 萤火虫

萤火虫对繁星说道：
"学者说你们的光亮终将于某天消失。"
繁星对其置之不理。

5

The night opens the flowers in secret and allows the day to get thanks.

黑夜静静地把花儿绽放了,
却让给了白日去领受谢词。

6

The leaf becomes flower when it loves. The flower becomes fruit when it worships[1].

热词天地

1.worship ['wɜːʃɪp] v. 崇拜,尊崇;热爱;爱慕

叶儿恋爱时便成了花儿。
花儿爱慕时便成了果儿。

7

The evening sky to me is like a window,
and a lighted lamp, and a waiting behind it.

在我看来,夜晚的天空,恍如一扇窗,
一盏明灯和它背后的守候。

8

When the sun goes down to the West,
the East of his morning stands before him in silence.

当夕阳西下,
黎明的东方已静悄悄地站在它的面前。

9

Maiden, your simplicity[1],
like the blueness of the lake,
reveals your depth of truth.

热词天地

1. simplicity [sɪmˈplɪsɪtɪ] *n.* 朴素；简易；天真；无知

少女啊，你的纯朴，
犹如湖水的碧蓝，
映射出你真实的深度。

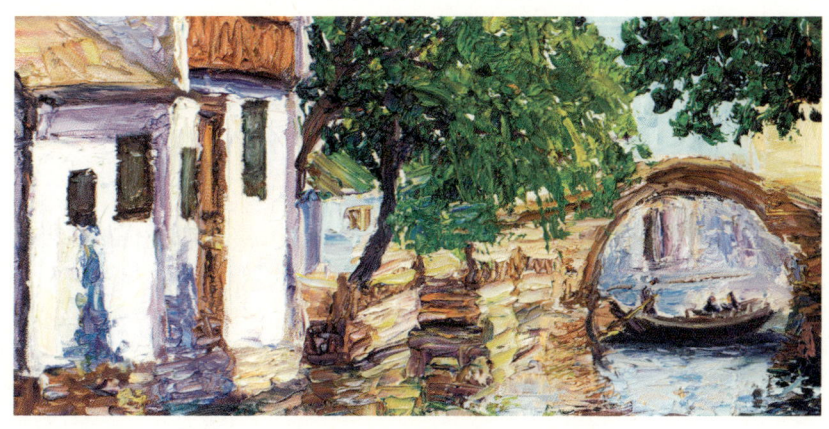

10

My evening came among the alien[1] trees and spoke in a language which my morning stars did not know.

热词天地

1.alien ['eɪlɪən] *adj.* 外国的；相异的，性质不同的；不相容的

我的夜色从奇异的树林中走来，
说着我的晨星所不懂的话语。

11

Night's darkness is a bag that bursts[1] with the gold of the dawn.

热词天地

1.burst [bɜːst] *vi.* 爆发，突发；爆炸

夜的漆黑宛如一只口袋，闪耀出晨曦的金色光芒。

12

Do not say,"It is morning", and dismiss[1] it with a name of yesterday.

See it for the first time as a newborn child that has no name.

热词天地

1.dismiss [dɪsˈmɪs] **vt.** 解雇，把……免职；遣散，解散（队伍等）；驳回，拒绝受理；搁置　**vi.** 解散

不要说"这是清晨"，也别用"昨天"这个名字来打发它。

初次见它，把它当做还没有名字的新生儿吧。

13

Find your beauty, my heart,
from the world's movement,
like the boat that has the grace[1] of the wind and the water.

热词天地

1.grace [greɪs] *n.* 优雅；恩惠；魅力；慈悲

我的心啊，
从世界的流动中寻找你的美吧，
正如那小舟兼具风与水的优雅风度。

14

Our desire lends the colours of the rainbow
to the mere mists and vapours[1] of life.

热词天地

1.vapour ['veɪpə] *n.* 蒸气（等于 vapor）；水蒸气

我们的渴望把彩虹的缤纷
借给了那云雾飘渺的人生。

15

The bird-song is the echo of the morning light back from the earth.

鸟啼是晨光返回大地的回音。

16

"Are you too proud to kiss me?"
the morning light asks the buttercup.

曙光问金凤花道：
"你真的不屑于亲吻我吗？"

17

If you shed tears when you miss the sun,
you also miss the stars.

如果在失去太阳时你流了泪，
那么你也将失去群星。

18

I came to your shore as a stranger,
I lived in your house as a guest,
I leave your door as a friend, my earth.

大地啊,我作为一个陌生人到达你的堤岸;
我作为房客住进你屋中;
我作为朋友离开你的房门。

19

The silent night has the beauty of the mother
and the clamorous[1] day of the child.

热词天地

1.clamorous ['klæmərəs] *adj.* 吵闹的;大声要求的

静谧的夜晚有着母亲般的美丽,
而喧闹的白天有着孩童般的可爱。

20

I dream of a star, an island of light,
where I shall be born
and in the depth of its quickening leisure[1]
my life will ripen its works like the rice-field in the autumn sun.

热词天地

1.leisure ['leʒə] *n.* 闲暇；空闲；安逸

我梦到了一颗星，一座光明岛屿，
我将在那里出生。
在它跃动的闲适深处，
我的生命将促使它事业成熟，就像秋日里的稻田。

21

I have scaled the peak and found
no shelter[1] in fame's bleak and barren[2] height.
Lead me, my Guide, before the light fades,
into the valley of quiet
where life's harvest mellows[3] into golden wisdom.

热词天地

1. shelter ['ʃeltə] *n.* 庇护；避难所；遮盖物
2. barren ['bærən] *adj.* 贫瘠的；无益的；沉闷无趣的
3. mellow ['meləʊ] *vt.* 使成熟；使柔和　*vi.* 成熟；变柔和

我曾攀上高峰并发现，
名誉的无趣和暗淡在那里无处遮掩。
指引我吧，我的向导，在光明消逝之前，
引我到幽静的山谷里去。
在那里，生命的收获将会成熟为金色的智慧。

流萤集

1

The jasmine's lisping of love to the sun is her flowers.

茉莉的花
便是她说给太阳的私密情话。

2

The tyrant claims freedom to kill freedom
and yet to keep it for himself.

暴君要求随意扼杀自由的权力,
却将自由只留给他自己。

3

Clouds are hills in vapour,
hills are clouds in stone,—
a phantasy in time's dream.

云朵是水汽凝成的山岗，
山岗是磐石铸就的云朵，——
这是时光梦境中的一支幻想曲。

4

The one without second is emptiness,
the other one makes it true.

独一无二只是虚幻，
一因有二才变得丰实。

5

The first flower that blossomed on this earth
was an invitation to the unborn song.

开在这地上的第一朵花
是对那未来的歌发出的邀请。

6

Dawn—the many-coloured flower—fades,
and then the simple light-fruit,
the sun appears.

黎明——这五色缤纷的花朵——
渐渐凋谢了，
于是那素朴的光明果实，太阳便
随即而来。

7

The inner world rounded in my life like a fruit matured in joy and sorrow,
will drop into the darkness of the original soil
for some further course of creation.

我生命的内在世界如同一枚果实，
在悲喜之中臻于圆熟，
它将会坠入黑暗的故土，
融进未来的造物宏图。

8

The razor-blade is proud of its keenness when it sneers at the sun.

剃刀对太阳冷笑，
它以锋利自居。

9

The muscle that has a doubt of its wisdom
throttles the voice that would cry.

肌肉怀疑自身的智慧,
因此扼住了即将发出的呼喊。

10

Life's play is swift,
life's play things fall behind one by one
and are forgotten.

生命的戏剧转瞬收场,
生命的玩具一件件遗落,
然后便被人遗忘。

11

Like my heart's pain that has long missed its meaning,
the sun's rays robed in dark
hide themselves under the ground.
Like my heart's pain at love's sudden touch,
they change their veil at the spring's call
and come out in the carnival of colours,
in flowers and leaves.

仿佛我心中
那早已忘却意义的苦痛,
披着黑暗衣裳的阳光
将自己藏进地底;
仿佛我心中
那突然被爱触动的苦痛,
阳光为了春天的召唤摘下面纱,
换上花叶织就的华衣,
出现在色彩的狂欢里。

 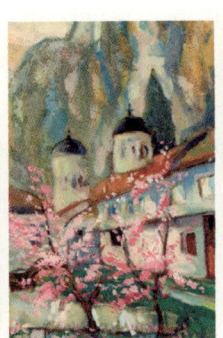 

12

Wealth is the burden of bigness,
welfare the fulness of being.

财富是显赫的负担,
幸福是存在的圆满。

13

Death laughs when the merit of the dead is exaggerated
for it swells his store with more than he can claim.

当人们吹嘘死者的美德,死亡便笑声朗朗,
因为他的库藏,藉份外之物而得膨胀。

14

The rainbow among the clouds may be great
but the little butterfly among the bushes is greater.

云间的彩虹可称奇观，
丛林中的小小蝴蝶却更加不凡。

15

The mist weaves her net round the morning
captivates him, and makes him blind.

朝雾织网笼住清晨，
迷住他，也迷了他的眼。

园丁集 （冰心译）

Let None Go back Home, Brothers

Over the green and yellow rice-fields sweep the shadows of the autumn clouds followed by the swift[1] chasing sun.
The bees forget to sip their honey; drunken with light they foolishly hover[2] and hum.

The ducks in the islands of the river clamour in joy for mere nothing.
Let none go back home, brothers, this morning, let none go to work.
Let us take the blue sky by storm and plunder[3] space as we run.

Laughter floats in the air like foam on the flood.
Brothers, let us squander[4] our morning in futile songs.

热词天地

1.swift [swɪft] *adj.* 快的；迅速的；敏捷的；立刻的 *adv.* 迅速地
2.hover ['hɒvə] *vi.* 盘旋，翱翔；徘徊 *vt.* 孵；徘徊在……近旁
3.plunder ['plʌndə] *n.* 抢夺；战利品；掠夺品 *vt.* 掠夺；抢劫 *vi.* 掠夺；盗窃
4.squander ['skwɒndə] *vt.* 浪费 *vi.* 浪费；漂泊

我们都不回家吧,兄弟们

黄绿的稻田上掠过秋云的阴影,后面是狂追的太阳。
蜜蜂被光明所陶醉,忘记吸蜜,只痴呆地飞翔嗡唱。

河里岛上的鸭群,无缘无故地欢乐地吵闹。
我们都不回家吧,兄弟们,今天早晨我们都不去工作。
让我们以狂风暴雨之势占领青天,让我们飞奔着抢夺空间吧。

笑声飘浮在空气上,像洪水上的泡沫。
弟兄们,让我们把清晨浪费在无用的歌曲上面吧。

O My Bird

Though the evening comes with slow steps and has signalled[1] for all songs to cease;
Though your companions have gone to their rest and you are tired;
Though fear broods in the dark and the face of the sky is veiled;
Yet, bird, O my bird, listen to me, do not close your wings.

That is not the gloom[2] of the leaves of the forest, that is the sea swelling like a dark black snake.
That is not the dance of the flowering jasmine[3], that is flashing foam.
Ah, where is the sunny green shore, where is your nest?
Bird, O my bird, listen to me, do not close your wings.
The lone night lies along your path, the dawn sleeps behind the shadowy hills.
The stars hold their breath counting the hours, the feeble moon swims the deep night.
Bird, O my bird, listen to me, do not close your wings.

There is no hope, no fear for you
There is no word, no whisper, no cry.
There is no home, no bed for rest.
There is only your own pair of wings and the pathless sky.
Bird, O my bird, listen to me, do not close your wings.

热词天地

1. signal ['sɪgnəl] *adj.* 暗示的；告知的 *v.* 标志着；给……发信号
2. gloom [gluːm] *n.* 忧郁；阴暗
3. jasmine ['dʒæzmɪn] *n.* 茉莉；淡黄色

啊，我的鸟儿

虽然夜晚缓步走来，让一切歌声停歇；
虽然你的伙伴都去休息而你也倦乏了；
虽然恐怖在黑暗中弥漫，天空的脸也被面纱遮起；
但是，鸟儿，我的鸟儿，听我的话，不要垂翅吧。

这不是林中树叶的阴影，这是大海涨溢，像一条深黑的龙蛇。
这不是盛开的茉莉花的舞姿，这是闪光的水沫。
啊，何处是阳光下的绿岸，何处是你的窝巢？
鸟儿，啊，我的鸟儿，听我的话，不要垂翅吧。
长夜躺在你的路边，黎明在朦胧的山后睡眠。
星辰屏息地数着时间，柔弱的月儿在夜中浮泛。
鸟儿，啊，我的鸟儿，听我的话，不要垂翅吧。

对于你，这里没有希望，没有恐怖。
这里没有消息，没有低语，没有呼唤。
这里没有家，没有休息的床。
这里只有你自己的一双翅翼和无路的天空。
鸟儿，啊，我的鸟儿，听我的话，不要垂翅吧。

I Was Walking by the Road

I was walking by the road, I do not know why, when the noonday was past and bamboo branches rustled in the wind.

The prone shadows with their outstretched arms clung to the feet of the hurrying light.

The koels were weary of their songs.

I was walking by the road, I do not know why.

The hut by the side of the water is shaded by an overhanging tree.

Someone was busy with her work, and her bangles made music in the corner.

I stood before this hut, I know not why.

The narrow winding road crosses many a mustard field, and many a mango forest.

It passes by the temple of the village and the market at the river landing place.

I stopped by this but, I do not know why.

Years age it was a day of breezy March when the murmur if the spring was languorous, and mango blossoms were dropping on the dust.

The rippling water leapt and licked the brass vessel that stood on the landing step.

I think of that day of breezy March, I do not know why.

Shadows are deepening and cattle returning to their folds.

The light is grey upon the lonely meadows, and the village are waiting for the ferry at the bank.

I slowly return upon my steps, I do not know why.

我在路边行走

我在路边行走，也不知道为什么，时已过午，竹枝在风中簌簌作响。
横斜的影子伸臂拖住流光的双足。
布谷鸟都唱倦了。
我在路边行走，也不知道为什么。

低垂的树荫盖住水边的茅屋。
有人正忙着工作，她的钏镯在角落里叮当作响。
我在茅屋前面站着，我不知道为什么。

曲径穿过一片芥菜田地和几层芒果树林。
它经过村庙和渡头的市集。
我在这茅屋面前停住了，我不知道为什么。

好几年前，三月风吹的一天，春天倦慵地低语，芒果花落在地上。
浪花跳起掠过立在渡头阶沿上的铜瓶。
我想着三月风吹的这一天，我不知道为什么。

阴影更深，牛群归栏。
冷落的牧场上日色苍白，村人在河边待渡。
我缓步回去，我不知道为什么。

Our Love Is Simple as a Song

Hands cling to hands and eyes linger on eyes; thus begins the record of our hearts.

It is the moonlit night of March; the sweet smell of henna is in the air; my flute lies on the earth neglected and your garland of flowers is unfinished.

This love between you and me is simple as a song.

Your veil of the saffron colour makes my eyes drunk.

The jasmine wreath that you wove me thrills to my heart like praise.

It is a game of giving and withholding, revealing and screening again; some smiles and some little shyness, and some sweet useless struggles.

This love between you and me is simple as a song.

No mystery beyond the present; no striving for the impossible; no shadow behind the charm; no groping in the depth of the dark.

This love between you and me is simple as a song.

We do not stray out of all words into the ever silent; we do not raise our hands to the void for things beyond hope.

It is enough what we give and we get.

We have not crushed the joy to the utmost to wring from it the wine of pain.

This love between you and me is simple as a song.

我们的爱像歌曲一样地单纯

手握着手,眼恋着眼;这样开始了我们的心的纪录。

这是三月的月明之夜;空气里有凤仙花的芬芳;我的横笛抛在地上,你的花串也没有编成。

你我之间的爱像歌曲一样地单纯。

你橙黄色的面纱使我眼睛陶醉。

你给我编的茉莉花环使我心震颤,像是受了赞扬。

这是一个又予又留、又隐又现的游戏;有些微笑,有些娇羞,也有些甜柔的无用的抵拦。

你我之间的爱像歌曲一样地单纯。

没有现在以外的神秘;不强求那做不到的事情;没有魅惑后面的阴影;没有黑暗深处的探索。

你我之间的爱像歌曲一样地单纯。

我们没有走出一切语言之外进入永远的沉默;我们没有向空举手寻求希望以外的东西。

我们付与,我们取得,这就够了。

我们没有把喜乐压成微尘来榨取痛苦之酒。

你我之间的爱像歌曲一样地单纯。

Her Name Is Ranjana

The yellow birds sing in their tree and make my heart dance with gladness.

We both live in the same village, and that is our one piece of joy.

Her pair of pet lambs come to graze in the shade of our garden trees.

If they stray into my barley field, I take them up in my arms.

The name of our village is Khanjana, and Anjana they call our river.

My name is known to all the village, and her name is Ranjana.

Only one field lies between us.

Bees that have hived in our grove go to seek honey in theirs.

Flowers launched from their landing-stairs come floating by the stream where we bathe.

Baskets of dried kusm flowers come from their fields to our market.

The name of our village is Khanjana, and Anjana they call our river.

My name is known to all the village, and her name is Ranjana.

The lane that winds to their house is fragrant in the spring with mango flowers.

When their linseed is ripe for harvest the hemp is in bloom in our field.

The stars that smile on their cottage send us the same twinkling look.

The rain that floods their tank makes glad our kadam forest.

The name of our village is Khanjana, and Anjana they call our river.

My name is known to all the village, and her name is Ranjana.

她的名字是软遮那

黄鸟在自己的树上歌唱，使我的心喜舞。
我们两人住在一个村子里，这是我们的一份快乐。
她心爱的一对小羊，到我园里树荫下吃草。
它们若走进我的麦地，我就把它们抱在臂里。
我们的村子名叫康遮那，人们管我们的小河叫安遮那。
我的名字村人都知道，她的名字是软遮那。

我们中间只隔着一块田地。
在我们树里做窝的蜜蜂，飞到他们林中去采蜜。
从他们渡头街上流来的落花，飘到我们洗澡的池塘里。
一筐一筐的红花干从他们地里送到我们的市集上。
我们村子名叫康遮那，人们管我们的小河叫安遮那。
我的名字村人都知道，她的名字是软遮那。

到她家去的那条曲巷，春天充满了芒果的花香。
他们亚麻子成熟的时候，我们地里的大麻正在开放。
在他们房上微笑的星辰，送给我们以同样的闪亮。
在他们水槽里满溢的雨水，也使我们的迦昙树林喜乐。
我们村子名叫康遮那，人们管我们的小河叫安遮那。
我的名字村人都知道，她的名字是软遮那。

When They Reach This Spot

When the two sisters go to fetch water, they come to this spot and they smile.

They must be aware of somebody who stands behind the trees whenever they go to fetch water.

The sisters whisper to each other when they pass this spot.

They must have guessed the secret of that somebody who stands behind the trees whenever they go to fetch water.

Their pitchers lurch suddenly, and water spills when they reach this spot.

They must have found that somebody's heart is beating who stands behind the trees whenever they go to fetch water.

The two sisters glance at each other when they come to this spot, and they smile.

There is a laughter in their swift-stepping feet, which make confusion in somebody's mind who stands behind the trees whenever they go to fetch water.

当她们走到这地点的时候

当这两个姊妹出去打水的时候,她们来到这地点,她们微笑了。
她们一定觉察到,每次她们出来打水的时候,那个站在树后的人儿。

姊妹俩相互耳语,当她们走过这地点的时候。
她们一定猜到了,每逢她们出来打水的时候,那个人站在树后的秘密。

她们的水瓶忽然倾倒,水倒出来了,当她们走到这地点的时候。
她们一定发觉,每逢她们出来打水的时候,那个站在树后的人的心正在跳着。

姊妹俩相互瞥了一眼又微笑了,当她们来到这地点的时候。
她们飞快的脚步里带着笑声,使这个每逢她们出来打水的时候站在树后的人儿心魂撩乱了。

Why Did You Peep at Me?

You walked by the riverside path with the full pitcher upon your hip.

Why did you swiftly turn your face and peep at me through your fluttering veil?

That gleaming look from the dark came upon me like a breeze that sends a shiver through the sipping water and sweeps away to the shadowy shore.

It came to me like a bird of the evening that hurriedly flies across the lampless room from the one open window to the other, and disappears in the night.

You are hidden like a star behind the hills, and I am a passer-by upon the road.

But why did you stop for a moment and glance at my face through your veil while you walked by the riverside path with the full pitcher upon your hip?

你为什么偷偷地看我?

你腰间搂着灌满的水瓶,在河边路上行走。
你为什么急遽地回头,从飘扬的面纱里偷偷地看我?

这个从黑暗中向我送来的闪视,像凉风在粼粼的微波上掠过,一阵震颤直到阴荫的岸边。

它向我飞来,像夜中的小鸟急遽地穿过无灯的屋子的两边洞开的窗户,又在黑夜中消失了。

你像一颗隐在山后的星星,我是路上的行人。
但是你为什么站了一会,从面纱中瞥视我的脸,当你腰间搂着灌满的水瓶在河边路上行走的时候?

He Only Comes and Goes Away

Day after day he comes and goes away.
Go, and give him a flower from my hair, my friend.
If he asks who was it that sent it, I entreat you do not tell him my name—for he only comes and goes away.

He sits on the dust under the tree.
Spread there a seat with flowers and leaves, my friend.
His eyes are sad, and they bring sadness to my heart.
He does not speak what he has in mind; he only comes and goes away.

他只是来了又走了

他天天来了又走了。

去吧,把我头上的花朵送去给他吧,我的朋友。

假如他问赠花的人是谁,我请你不要把我的名字告诉他——因为他来了又要走的。

他坐在树下的地上。

用繁花密叶给他铺设一个座位吧,我的朋友。

他的眼神是忧郁的,它把忧郁带到我的心中。

他没有说出他的心事;他只是来了又走了。

Why Did He Choose to Come My Door?

Why did he choose to come to my door, the wandering youth, when the day dawned?

As I come in and out I pass by him every time, and my eyes are caught by his face.

I know not if I should speak to him or keep silent. Why did he choose to come to my door.

The cloudy nights in July are dark; the sky is soft blue in the autumn; the spring days are restless with the south wind.

He weaves his songs with fresh tunes every time.

I turn from my work and my eyes fill with the mist. Why did he choose to come my door?

他为什么特地来到我的门前?

他为什么特地来到我的门前,这年轻的游子,在黎明时分?
每次我进出经过他的身旁,我的眼睛总被他的面庞所吸引。
我不知道我是应该同他说话还是保持沉默。他为什么特地到我门前来呢?

七月的阴夜是黑沉的;秋日的天空是浅蓝的;南风把春天吹得骀荡不宁。
他每次用新调编着新歌。
我放下活计眼里充满雾水。他为什么特地到我门前来呢?

Why There Is Madness in Your Eyes?

"Come to us, youth, tell us truly why there is madness in your eyes?"

"I know not what wine of wild poppy I have drunk, that there is this madness in my eyes."

"Ah, shame!"

"Well, some are wise and some foolish, some are watchful and some careless. There are eyes that smile and eyes that weep—and madness is in my eyes."

"Youth, why do you stand so still under the shadow of the tree?"

"My feet are languid with the burden of my heart, and I stand still in the shadow."

"Ah, shame!"

"Well, some march on their way and some linger, some are free and some are fettered—and my feet are languid with the burden of my heart."

为什么你眼里带着疯癫?

"到我们这里来吧,青年人,老实告诉我们,为什么你眼里带着疯癫?"
"我不知道我喝了什么野罂粟花酒,使我的眼里带着疯癫。"
"呵,多难为情!"
"好吧,有的人聪明有的人愚拙,有的人细心有的人马虎。有的眼睛会笑,有的眼睛会哭——我的眼睛是带着疯癫的。"

"青年人,你为什么这样凝立在树影下呢?"
"我的脚被我沉重的心压得疲倦了,我就在树影下凝立着。"
"呵,多难为情!"
"好吧,有人一直行进,有人到处流连,有的人是自由的,有的人是被束缚的——我的脚被我沉重的心压得疲倦了。"

吉檀迦利 （冰心 译）

Light

Light, my light, the world-filling light, the eye-kissing light, heart-sweetening light!

Ah, the light dances, my darling, at the centre of my life; the light strikes, my darling, the chords[1] of my love; the sky opens, the wind runs wild, laughter passes over the earth.

The butterflies spread their sails on the sea of light. Lilies and jasmines surge up on the crest of the waves of light.

The light is shattered into gold on every cloud, my darling, and it scatters[2] gems in profusion.

Mirth spreads from leaf to leaf, my darling, and gladness without measure. The heaven's river has drowned its banks and the flood of joy is abroad.

热词天地

1. chord [kɔ:d] *n.* （乐器）弦；

2. scatter ['skætə] *vi.* 分散，散开；散射

光明

光明,我的光明,充满世界的光明,吻着眼目的光明,甜沁心腑的光明!

呵,我的宝贝,光明在我生命的一角跳舞;我的宝贝,光明在勾拨我爱的心弦;天开了,大风狂奔,笑声响彻大地。

蝴蝶在光明的海上展开翅帆。百合与茉莉在光波的浪花上翻涌。

我的宝贝,光明在每朵云彩上散映成金,它洒下大量的珠宝。

我的宝贝,快乐在树叶间伸展,欢喜无边。天河的堤岸已被淹没,欢乐的洪水在四散奔流。

Clouds

Thy sunbeam[1] comes upon this earth of mine with arms outstretched and stands at my door the livelong day to carry back to thy feet clouds made of my tears and sighs and songs.

With fond delight thou wrappest about thy starry breast that mantle[2] of misty cloud, turning it into numberless shapes and folds and colouring it with hues everchanging.

It is so light and so fleeting[3], tender and tearful and dark, that is why thou lovest it. O,thou spotless and serene. And that is why it may cover thy awful white light with its pathetic[4] shadows.

热词天地

1.sunbeam ['sʌnbi:m] *n.* 阳光，日光；快乐的人
2.mantle ['mænt(ə)l] *n.* 地幔；斗篷；覆盖物　*vi.* 覆盖；脸红　*vt.* 覆盖
3.fleeting ['fli:tɪŋ] *adj.* 飞逝的；转瞬间的
4.pathetic [pə'θetɪk] *adj.* 可怜的，悲哀的；感伤的；乏味的

云彩

你的阳光射到我的地上,整天的伸臂站在我门前,把我的眼泪,叹息和歌曲变成的云彩,带回放在你的足边。

你喜爱地将这云带缠围在你的星胸之上,绕成无数的形式和褶纹,还染上变幻无穷的色彩。

它是那样的轻柔,那样地飘扬、温软、含泪而黯淡,因此你就爱惜它,呵,你这庄严无瑕者。这就是为什么它能够以它可怜的阴影遮掩你的可畏的白光。

Roaming Cloud

I am like a remnant of a cloud of autumn uselessly roaming in the sky.O,my sun ever-glorious! Thy touch has not yet melted[1] my vapour, making me one with thy light, and thus I count months and years separated from thee.

If this be thy wish and if this be thy play, then take this fleeting emptiness of mine, paint it with colours, gild it with gold, float it on the wanton[2] wind and spread it in varied wonders.

And again when it shall be thy wish to end this play at night, I shall melt and vanish away in the dark, or it may be in a smile of the white morning, in a coolness of purity transparent[3].

热词天地

1.melt [melt] *v.* 融化；溶解
2.wanton ['wɒntən] *adj.* 嬉戏的；繁茂的；荒唐的
3.transparent [træn'spærənt] *adj.* 透明的；显然的；坦率的；
　separate from 分离；把……和……分开

浮云

我像一片秋天的残云,无主地在空中飘荡,呵,我的永远光耀的太阳!你的摩触还没有蒸化了我的水气,使我与你的光明合一,因此我计算着和你分离的悠长的年月。

假如这是你的愿望,假如这是你的游戏,就请把我这流逝的空虚染上颜色,镀上金辉,让它在狂风中飘浮,舒卷成种种的奇观。

而且假如你愿意在夜晚结束这场游戏,我就在黑暗中,或在灿白晨光的微笑中,在净化的清凉中,溶化消失。

Lotus

On the day when the lotus bloomed, alas, my mind was straying[1], and I knew it not. My basket was empty and the flower remained unheeded[2].

Only now and again a sadness fell upon me, and I started up from my dream and felt a sweet trace[3] of a strange fragrance in the south wind.

That vague sweetness made my heart ache with longing and it seemed to me that it was the eager breath of the summer seeking for its completion.

I knew not then that it was so near, that it was mine, and that this perfect sweetness had blossomed in the depth of my own heart.

热词天地

1.stray [streɪ] *vi.* 流浪；迷路；偏离　*adj.* 迷路的；离群的；偶遇的
2.unheeded [ʌnˈhiːdɪd] *adj.* 被忽视的；未被注意的
3.trace [treɪs] *vt.* 追踪，查探；描绘；回溯　*n.* 痕迹，踪迹
　 start up 开始；发动；突然站起；突然出现

莲花

莲花开放的那天,唉,我不自觉的在心魂飘荡。我的花篮空着,花儿我也没有去理睬。

不时的有一段幽愁来袭击我,我从梦中惊起,觉得南风里有一阵奇香的芳踪。

这迷茫的温馨,使我想望得心痛,我觉得这仿佛是夏天渴望的气息,寻求圆满。

我那时不晓得它离我是那么近,而且是我的,这完美的温馨,还是在我自己心灵的深处开放。

新月集

The Banyan Tree

O you shaggy-headed banyan tree standing on the bank of the pond, have you forgotten the little child, like the birds that have nested in your branches and left you?

Do you not remember how he sat at the window and wondered at the tangle¹ of your roots that plunged² underground?

The women would come to fill their jars in the pond, and your huge black shadow would wriggle on the water like sleep struggling to wake up.

Sunlight danced on the ripples³ like restless tiny shuttles weaving golden tapestry.

Two ducks swam by the weedy⁴ margin above their shadows, and the child would sit still and think.

He longed to be the wind and blow through your rustling branches, to be your shadow and lengthen with the day on the water, to be a bird

and perch on your top-most twig, and to float like those ducks among the weeds and shadows.

热词天地

1. tangle ['tæŋgl] *n.* 纠纷；混乱状态
2. plunge [plʌndʒ] *v.* 颠簸；暴跌；骤降
3. ripple ['rɪpl] *n.* 涟漪；波纹
4. weedy ['wi:dɪ] *adj.* 瘦弱的；似杂草的；尽是杂草的
   wake up 醒来，起床；开始警觉；开始了解真相

榕树

喂,你,站在池边的枝叶蓬乱的榕树,你是不是已经忘记了那小小的孩子,那在你的枝上筑巢又离开了你的鸟儿似的孩子?

你还记得他怎样坐在窗内,惊讶于你纠缠那深入地下的树根吗?

妇人们常到池边,来汲满罐的水,这时你巨大的黑影便在水面上荡漾,好像睡着的人挣扎着要醒来似的。

日光在微波上跳舞,好像不停息的小梭子在织着金色的花毡。

两只鸭子挨着芦苇,在池中芦苇的倒影上游来游去,孩子静静地坐在那里思索。

他想做风,吹过你飒飒的枝丫;想做你的影子,在水面上随着日光而消长;想做一只鸟儿,栖息在你的最高枝上;还想做那两只鸭,在芦苇与阴影中游来游去。

第三卷 旅途

飞鸟集

1

Stray birds of summer come to my window to sing and fly away. And yellow leaves of autumn, which have no songs, flutter[1] and fall there with a sign.

热词天地

1.flutter ['flʌtə] vi. 飘动；鼓翼；烦扰
   vt. 拍；使焦急；使飘动

夏鸟飞临我窗前，歌唱着，又离去了。
秋叶无曲吟唱，凋零在地上。
只一声叹息。

2

There little thoughts are the rustle of leaves; they have their whisper of joy in my mind.

这些凌乱的思绪，仿佛飒飒的树叶声；
它们在我的心间，快乐地呢喃着。

3

My day is done, and I am like a boat drawn on the beach, listening to the dance-music of the tide[1] in the evening.

热词天地

1.tide [taɪd] *n.* 趋势，潮流；潮汐

我的白日时光已尽，
我形同一只停泊在海滩上的小船，
在夜里倾听着潮汐鸣奏的舞曲。

4

Take my wine in my own cup, friend.
It loses its wreath[1] of foam[2] when poured into that of others.

热词天地

1. wreath [ri:θ] *n.* 花冠；圈状物
2. foam [fəʊm] *n.* 泡沫；气泡；泡沫产品，泡沫剂

快畅饮了我杯中的美酒吧，朋友。
倘若将它倒进别人的杯中，这美酒升腾起的泡沫将会消失。

5

Be still, my heart, these great trees are prayers.

沉静些吧,我的心,
这些参天大树都是祈福者啊!

6

I carry in my world that flourishes the worlds that have failed.

我把那些昔世的浮华带进了我的世界。

7

Dear friend, I feel the silence of your great thoughts of many a deepening eventide[1] on this beach when I listen to these waves.

热词天地
1.eventide ['i:vntaɪd] *n.* 黄昏；日暮

亲爱的朋友啊，当我静听着海涛时，
我感觉到你光辉思想的静谧，
就在这夜色朦胧的海滩上。

8

This rainy evening the wind is restless. I look at the swaying branches and ponder over the greatness of all things.

热词天地
ponder over 深思，沉思；考虑

在风雨飘摇的黄昏，
我望着摇曳不定的树枝，
思考着世间万物的伟大。

9

Let me think that there is one among those stars
that guides my life through the dark unknown.

不妨这样设想，璀璨夜空中有一颗星，
指引着我的生命穿过这未知的黑暗。

10

Thoughts pass in my mind like flocks[1] of ducks in the sky.
I hear the voice of their wings.

热词天地

1.flock [flɒk] *n.* 群；大堆，大量

思绪划过我的脑海，像一群野鸭掠过天空。
我听见了它们振翅的声音。

11

Thou hast led me through my crowded¹ travels of the day to my evening's loneliness.
I wait for its meaning through the stillness of the night.

热词天地

1.crowded ['kraʊdɪd] *adj.* 拥挤的；塞满的

您曾带着我穿过白天那熙熙攘攘的旅途，
来到黄昏这孤寂之处。
在夜的沉静里，我等待着它的意义。

12

Thought feeds itself with its own words and grows.

思想用自己的言语喂养着自己而成长着。

13

I am like the road in the night listening to the footfalls of its memories in silence.

我仿佛像那夜里的小径,
静静地聆听记忆的足音。

14

I am the autumn cloud, empty of rain,
see my fullness in the field of ripened rice.

我是秋云，空洞无雨，
但在成熟的稻田里，却可看到我的殷殷奉献。

15

My sad thoughts tease[1] me asking me their own names.

热词天地

1.tease [ti:z] *vt.* 取笑；戏弄；梳理；欺负；强求

我的伤感萦绕着我，一再问我它们自己的名字。

16

Things look fantastic[1] in this dimness[2] of the dusk—
the spires whose bases are lost in the dark
and tree tops like blots of ink.
I shall wait for the morning
and wake up to see thy city in the light.

热词天地

1.fantastic [fæn'tæstɪk] *adj.* 奇异的；古怪的；极好的，不可思议的
2.dimness ['dɪmnɪs] *n.* 微暗；不清楚；混沌

在这薄暮的朦胧之中，一切都如梦似幻——
尖塔的基底消失在了黑暗中，
树冠也仿佛墨迹斑斑。
我将等待黎明，
并在醒来时看见你光明的城市。

17

I have sung the songs of thy day.
In the evening let me carry thy lamp
through the stormy path.

我已唱过了您的白日恋歌。
傍晚时分,就让我捧着您的灯,
走完那风雨飘摇的旅途吧。

18

I am in the world of the roads.
The night comes. Open thy gate,
thou world of the home.

我在道路错综的世界上。
夜来了。打开您的门吧,
那是您家的世界啊!

流萤集

1

Darkness is the veiled bride
silently waiting for the errant light
to return to her bosom.

黑夜是蒙着面纱的新娘，
静静等待那跳跃的光明
重回她的怀抱。

2

Trees are the earth's endless effort to speak to the listening heaven.

森林是大地向聆听的天空的无休止的
努力倾诉。

3

The burden of self is lightened when I laugh at myself.

当我嘲笑自身时,
自我的重负便由之缓解。

4

The weak can be terrible because they try furiously to appear strong.

弱者也会变得让人畏惧,
因为他们迫切地希望表现得强大。

5

The wind of heaven blows, the anchor desperately clutches the mud, and my boat is beating its breast against the chain.

天堂的风吹起,
锚拼命地抓紧泥浆,
而我的小船,则用胸膛紧靠着锚链。

6

My fancies are fireflies, —specks of living light twinkling in the dark.

我的幻想是一群萤火虫,——活跃的火花,在黑暗中闪烁。

7

With the ruins of terror's triumph children build their doll's house.

可怕的胜利已成残垣,
孩子们用它的碎片搭建了玩具房屋。

8

The lamp waits through the long day of neglect
for the flame's kiss in the night.

油灯度过漠然而漫长的白昼,
只为静候夜间火焰的亲吻。

9

Spring hesitates at winters door,
but the mango blossom rashly runs out to him
before her time and meets her doom.

春天在冬天的门前流连,
芒果花却等不及花期来临,
鲁莽地跑出去迎候,
于是迎来了自己的厄运。

10

My life's empty flute[1]
waits for its final music
like the primal darkness
before the stars came out.

热词天地

1.flute [fluːt] *n.* 长笛;(柱上的)凹槽 *v.* 吹长笛

我生命的空寂长笛
等待着它最后的乐章,
如同繁星闪现之前
那原本的深沉夜色。

11

Some have thought deeply and explored
the meaning of thy truth,
and they are great;
I have listened to catch the music of thy play,
and I am glad.

有人曾殚精竭虑，
探求你真理的意义，
他们了不起；
而我曾凝神聆听你演奏的乐曲，
我也满心欢喜。

12

The world is the ever-changing foam
that floats on the surface of a sea of silence.

世界是幻化无休的泡沫,
在沉默之海的表面随波漂流。

13

These paper boats of mine are meant to dance
on the ripples of hours,
and not to reach any destination.

我的这些小纸船
只想在时光的涟漪里凌波起舞,
却不想到达任何口岸。

14

God honoured me with his fight
when I was rebellious,
He ignored me when I was languid.

当我奋起反抗,神明赐我以他的打击,
当我颓然蛰伏,他又对我掉头不顾。

15

The sectarian thinks
that he has the sea
ladled into his private pond.

思想褊狭的人
自以为已经将整个海洋
舀进了自己的私家池塘。

16

In the shady depth of life
are the lonely nests of memories
that shrink from words.

躲避言辞的记忆，
在生命的幽暗深处
筑起一个个凄清的巢窠。

17

Let my love find its strength
in the service of day,
its peace in the union of night.

让我的爱从白昼的劳作中
找到力量，
从夜晚的和谐中找到安详。

园丁集 （冰心译）

To-day Is the Festival of Phantoms

To the guests that must go bid God's speed and brush away all traces of their steps. Take to your bosom with a smile what is easy and simple and near. To-day is the festival of phantoms[1] that know not when they die. Let your laughter be but a meaningless mirth[2] like twinkles of light on the ripples. Let your life lightly dance on the edges of time like dew on the tip of a leaf. Strike in chords from your harp[3] fitful momentary rhythms.

热词天地

1. phantom ['fæntəm] *n.* 幽灵；幻影；虚位
2. mirth [mɜ:θ] *n.* 欢笑；欢乐；高兴
3. harp [hɑ:p] *n.* 竖琴　　*vi.* 弹奏竖琴；喋喋不休；不停地说
   brush away 刷去

今天是幻影的节日

对那些定要离开的客人们,求神帮他们快走,并且扫除他们所有的足迹。

把舒服的、单纯的、亲近的微笑一起抱在你的怀里。

今天是幻影的节日,他们不知道自己的死期。

让你的笑声只作为无意义的欢乐,像浪花上的闪光。

让你的生命像露珠在叶尖一样,在时间的边缘上轻轻跳舞。

在你的琴弦上弹出无定的暂时的音调吧。

I Know You, Modest Mendicant

"What comes from your willing hands I take. I beg for nothing more."

"Yes, yes, I know you, modest mendicant, you ask for all that one has."

"If there be a stray flower for me I will wear it in my heart."
"But if there be thorns?"
"I will endure them."
"Yes, yes, I know you, modest mendicant, you ask for all that one has."

"If but once you should raise your loving eyes to my face it would make my life sweet beyond death."
"But if there be only cruel glances?"
"I will keep them piercing my heart."
"Yes, yes, I know you, modest mendicant, you ask for all that one has."

我懂得你,谦卑的乞丐

"从你慷慨的手里所付予的,我都接受。我别无所求。"
"是了,是了,我懂得你,谦卑的乞丐,你是乞求一个人的一切所有。"

"若是你给我一朵残花,我也要把它戴在心上。"
"若是那花上有刺呢?"
"我就忍受着。"
"是了,是了,我懂得你,谦卑的乞丐,你是乞求一个人的一切所有。"

"如果你只在我脸上瞥来一次爱怜的眼光,就会使我的生命直到死后还是甜蜜的。"
"假如那只是残酷的眼色呢?"
"我要让它永远穿刺我的心。"
"是了,是了,我懂得你,谦卑的乞丐,你是乞求一个人的一切所有。"

I Cannot Understand Them

"Trust love even if it brings sorrow. Do not close up your heart."
"Ah no, my friend, your words are dark, I cannot understand them."

"The heart is only giving away with a tear and a song, my love."
"Ah no, my friend, your words are dark, I cannot understand them."

"Pleasure is frail like a dewdrop, while it laughs it dies. But sorrow is strong and abiding. Let sorrowful love wake in your eyes."
"Ah no, my friend, your words are dark, I cannot understand them."

"The lotus blooms in the sight of the sun, and loses all that it has. It would not remain in bud in the eternal winter mist."
"Ah no, my friend, your words are dark, I cannot understand them."

我不懂得

"即使爱只给你带来了哀愁,也信任它。不要把你的心关起。"
"呵,不,我的朋友,你的话语太隐晦了,我不懂得。"

"心是应该和一滴眼泪、一首诗歌一起送给人的,我爱。"
"呵,不,我的朋友,你的话语太隐晦了,我不懂得。"

"喜乐像露珠一样地脆弱,它在欢笑中死去。哀愁却是坚强而耐久。让含愁的爱在你眼中醒起吧。"
"呵,不,我的朋友,你的话语太隐晦了,我不懂得。"

"荷花在日中开放,丢掉了自己的一切所有。在永生的冬雾里,它将不再含苞。"
"呵,不,我的朋友,你的话语太隐晦了,我不懂得。"

You Can Never Know It

Your questioning eyes are sad. They seem to know my meaning as the moon would fathom the sea.

I have bared my life before your eyes from end to end, with nothing hidden or held back. That is why you know me not.

If it were only a gem I could break it into a hundred pieces and string them into a chain to put on your neck.

If it were only a flower, round and small and sweet, I could pluck it from its stem to set it in your hair.

But it is a heart, my beloved. Where are its shores and its bottom?

You know not the limits of this kingdom, still you are its queen.

If it were only a moment of pleasure it would flower in an easy smile, and you could see it and read it in a moment.

If it were merely a pain it would melt in limpid tears, reflecting its inmost secret without a word.

But it is love, my beloved.

Its pleasure and pain are boundless, and endless its wants and wealth.

It is as near to you as your life, but you can never wholly know it.

你永远不能了解它

你的疑问的眼光是含愁的。它要追探了解我的意思,好像月亮探测大海。我已经把我生命的终始,全部暴露在你的眼前,没有任何隐秘和保留。因此你不认识我。

假如它是一块宝石,我就能把它碎成千百颗粒,穿成项链挂在你的颈上。
假如它是一朵花,圆圆小小香香的,我就能从枝上采来戴在你的发上。
但是它是一颗心,我的爱人。何处是它的边和底?
你不知道这个王国的边极,但你仍是这王国的女王。

假如它是片刻的欢娱,它将在喜笑中开花,你立刻就会看到、懂得了。
假如它是一阵痛苦,它将融化成晶莹的眼泪,不着一字地反映出它最深的秘密。
但是它是爱,我的爱人。
它的欢乐和痛苦是无边的,它的需求和财富是无尽的。
它和你亲近得像你的生命一样,但是你永远不能完全了解它。

Speak to Me

Speak to me, my love! Tell me in words what you sang.

The night is dark. The stars are lost in clouds. The wind is sighing through the leaves.

I will let loose my hair. My blue cloak will cling round me like night. I will clasp your head to my bosom; and there in the sweet loneliness murmur on your heart. I will shut my eyes and listen. I will not look in your face.

When your words are ended, we will sit still and silent. Only the trees will whisper in the dark.

The night will pale. The day will dawn. We shall look at each other's eyes and go on our different paths.

Speak to me, my love! Tell me in words what you sang.

对我说吧

对我说吧,我爱!用言语告诉我你唱的是什么。

夜是深黑的,星星消失在云里,风在叶丛中叹息。
我将披散我的头发,我的青蓝的披风将像黑夜一样地紧裹着我。我将把你的头紧抱在胸前:在甜柔的寂寞中在你心头低诉。我将闭目静听。我不会看望你的脸。

等到你的话说完了,我们将沉默凝坐。只有丛树在黑暗中微语。
夜将发白。天光将晓。我们将望望彼此的眼睛,然后各走各的路。

对我说话吧,我爱!用言语告诉我你唱的是什么。

You Are My Own

You are the evening cloud floating in the sky of my dreams.
I paint you and fashion you ever with my love longings.
You are my own, my own, Dweller in my endless dreams!

Your feet are rosy-red with the glow of my heart's desire, Gleaner of my sunset songs!
Your lips are bitter-sweet with the taste of my wine of pain.
You are my own, my own, Dweller in my lonesome dreams!

With the shadow of my passion have I darken your eyes, Haunter of the depth of my gaze!
I have caught you and wrapt you, my love, in the net of my music.
You are my own, my own, Dweller in my deathless dreams!

你是我一个人的

你是一朵夜云,在我梦幻中的天空浮泛。
我永远用爱恋的渴想来描画你。
你是我一个人的,我一个人的,我无尽的梦幻中的居住者!

你的双脚被我心切望的热光染得绯红,我的落日之歌的搜集者!
我的痛苦之酒使你的唇儿苦甜。
你是我一个人的,我一个人的,我寂寥的梦幻中的居住者!

我用热情的浓影染黑了你的眼睛;我的凝视深处的崇魂!
我捉住了你,缠住了你,我爱,在我音乐的罗网里。
你是我一个人的,我一个人的,我永生的梦幻中的居住者!

If This Be True

Tell me if this be all true, my lover, tell me if this be true.

When these eyes flash their lightning the dark clouds in your breast make stormy answer.

Is it true that my lips are sweet like the opening bud of the first conscious love?

Do the memories of vanished months of May linger in my limbs?

Does the earth, like a harp, shiver into songs with the touch of my feet?

Is it then true that the dewdrops fall from the eyes of night when I am seen, and the morning light is glad when it wraps my body round?

Is it true, is it true, that your love travelled alone through ages and worlds in search of me?

That when you found me at last, your age-long desire found utter peace in my gentle speech and my eyes and lips and flowing hair?

Is it then true that the mystery of the infinite is written on this little forehead of mine?

Tell me, my lover, if all this be true.

这是否真的

告诉我,这一切是否都是真的。我的情人,告诉我,这是否真的。

当这一对眼睛闪出电光,你胸中的浓云发出风暴的回答。
我的唇儿,是真像觉醒的初恋的蓓蕾那样香甜么?
消失了的五月的回忆仍旧流连在我的肢体上么?

那大地,像一张琴,真因着我双足的踏触而颤成诗歌么?
那么当我来时,从夜的眼睛里真的落下露珠,晨光也真因为围绕我的身躯而感到喜悦么?

是真的么,是真的么,你的爱贯穿许多时代、许多世界来寻找我么?
当你最后找到了我,你天长地久的渴望,在我的温柔的话里,在我的眼睛嘴唇和飘扬的头发里,找到了完全的宁静么?
那么无限的神秘是真的写在我小小的额上么?

告诉我,我的情人,这一切是否都是真的。

I Know Your Art

Lest I should know you too easily, you play with me.
You blind me with flashes of laughter to hide your tears.
I know, I know your art.
You never say the word you would.

Lest I should not prize you, you elude me in a thousand ways.
Lest I should confuse you with the crowd, you stand aside.
I know, I know your art.
You never walk the path you would.

Your claim is more than that of others, that is why you are silent.
With playful carelessness you avoid my gifts.
I know, I know your art.
You never will take what you would.

我知道你的妙计

只恐我太容易地认得你,你对我耍花招。
你用欢笑的闪光使我目盲来掩盖你的眼泪。
我知道,我知道你的妙计。
你从来不说出你所要说的话。

只恐我不珍爱你,你千方百计地闪避我。
只恐我把你和大家混在一起,你独自站在一边。
我知道,我知道你的妙计,
你从来不走你所要走的路。

你的要求比别人都多,因此你才静默。
你用嬉笑的无心来回避我的赠与。
我知道,我知道你的妙计,
你从来不肯接受你想接受的东西。

Why Does He Not Come?

He whispered, "My love, raise your eyes."
I sharply chid him, and said "Go!"; but he did not stir.

He stood before me and held both my hands. I said, "Leave me!"; but he did not go.

He brought his face near my ear. I glanced at him and said, "What a shame!"; but he did not move.

His lips touched my cheek. I trembled and said, "You dare too much"; but he had no shame.

He put a flower in my hair. I said, "It is useless!"; but he stood unmoved.

He took the garland from my neck and went away. I weep and ask my heart, "Why does he not come?"

他为什么不回来呢?

他低声说:"我爱,抬起眼睛吧。"
我严厉地责骂他说:"走!"但是他不动。

他站在我面前拉住我的双手。我说:"躲开我!"但是他没有走。
他把脸靠近我的耳边。我瞪他一眼说:"不要脸!"但是他没有动。

他的嘴唇触到我的腮颊。我震颤了,说:"你太大胆了!"但是他不怕丑。
他把一朵花插在我发上。我说:"这也没有用处!"但是他站着不动。

他取下我颈上的花环就走开了。我哭了,问我的心说:"他为什么不回来呢?"

My Heart Is Given to the Many

Would you put your wreath of fresh flowers on my neck, fair one?

But you must know that the one wreath that I had woven is for the many, for those who are seen in glimpses, or dwell in lands unexplored, or live in poets' songs.

It is too late to ask my heart in return for yours.

There was a time when my life was like a bud, all its perfume was stored in its core.

Now it is squandered far and wide.

Who knows the enchantment that can gather and shut it up again?

My heart is not mine to give to one only, it is given to the many.

我的心是要给与许多人的

你愿意把你的鲜花的花环挂在我的颈上么,佳人?
但是你要晓得,我编的那个花环,是为大家的,为那些偶然瞥见的人,住在未开发的大地上的人,住在诗人歌曲里的人。

现在来请求我的心作为答赠已经太晚了。
曾有一个时候,我的生命像一朵蓓蕾,它所有的芬芳都储藏在花心里。
现在它已远远地喷溢四散。

谁晓得有什么魅力,可以把它们收集关闭起来呢?
我的心不容我只给一个人,它是要给与许多人的。

My Love

My love, once upon a time your poet launched a great epic in his mind.

Alas, I was not careful, and it struck your ringing anklets and came to grief.

It broke up into scraps of songs and lay scattered at your feet.

All my cargo of the stories of old wars was tossed by the laughing waves and soaked in tears and sank.

You must make this loss good to me, my love.

If my claims to immortal fame after death are shattered, make me immortal while I live.

And I will not mourn for my loss nor blame you.

我爱

我爱,从前有一天,你的诗人把一首伟大史诗投进他心里。
呵,我不小心,它打到你的叮当的脚镯上而引起悲愁。
它裂成诗歌的碎片散洒在你的脚边。

我满载的一切古代战争的货物,都被笑浪所颠簸,被眼泪浸透而下沉。
你必须使这损失成为我的收获,我爱。

如果我的死后不朽的荣名的希望都破灭了,那就在生前使我不朽吧。
我将不为这损失伤心,也不责怪你。

I Am Tired

I spent my day on the scorching[1] hot dust of the road.
Now, in the cool of the evening, I knock at the door of the inn. It is deserted and in ruins.

A grim ashath tree spreads its hungry clutching roots through the gaping fissures[2] of the walls.

Days have been when wayfarers[3] came here to wash their weary feet.

They spread their mats in the courtyard in the dim light of the early moon, and sat and talked of strange lands.

They work refreshed in the morning when birds made them glad, and friendly flowers nodded their heads at them from the wayside.

But no lighted lamp awaited me when I came here.

The black smudges[4] of smoke left by many a forgotten evening lamp stare, like blind eyes, from the wall.

Fireflies flit in the bush near the dried-up pond, and bamboo branches fling their shadows on the grass-grown path.

I am the guest of no one at the end of my day.

The long night is before me, and I am tired.

热词天地

1. scorching ['skɔ:tʃɪŋ] *adj.* 灼热的；激烈的；讽刺的
2. fissure ['fɪʃə] *n.* 裂缝；裂沟（尤指岩石上的）
3. wayfarer ['weɪfeərə] *n.* 旅人，徒步旅行者
4. smudge [smʌdʒ] *n.* 污点，污迹；烟熏火堆
   in ruins 成为废墟；严重受损

我疲倦了

我在大路灼热的尘土上消磨了一天。
现在,在晚凉中,我敲着一座小庙的门。这庙已经荒废倒塌了。
一棵愁苦的菩提树,从破墙的裂缝里伸展出饥饿的爪根。

从前曾有过路人到这里来洗疲乏的脚。
他们在新月的微光中在院里摊开席子,坐着谈论异地的风光。
早起他们精神恢复了,鸟声使他们欢悦,友爱的花儿在道边向他们点首。
但是当我来的时候没有灯在等待我。
只有残留的灯烟熏污的黑迹,像盲人的眼睛,从墙上瞪视着我。
萤火虫在涸池边的草里闪烁,竹影在荒芜的小径上摇曳。
我在一天之末做了没有主人的客人。
在我面前的是漫漫的长夜,我疲倦了。

It Is Time to Come Home

Why do you sit there and jingle[1] your bracelets in mere idle sport?

Fill your pitcher. It is time for you to come home.

Why do you stir the water with your hands and fitfully[2] glance at the road for someone in mere idle sport?

Fill your pitcher and come home.

The morning hours pass by—the dark waters flows on.

The waves are laughing and whispering to each other in mere idle sport.

The wandering clouds have gathered at the edge of the sky on yonder rise of the land.

They linger[3] and look at your face and smile in mere idle sport.

Fill your pitcher and come home.

热词天地

1.jingle ['dʒɪŋgl] *n.* 叮当声 *v.* （使）叮当作响；具有简单而又引人注意的韵律
2.fitfully ['fɪtfəlɪ] *adv.* 断断续续地；发作地
3.linger ['lɪŋgə] *vi.* 徘徊；苟延残喘；磨蹭 *vt.* 消磨；缓慢度过
    glance at 看一下，浏览；提到，影射
    pass by 经过；走过；逝去

是回家的时候了

你为什么悠闲地坐在那里,把镯子玩得叮当作响呢?
把你的水瓶灌满了吧。是你应当回家的时候了。
你为什么悠闲地拨弄着水玩,偷偷地瞥视路上的行人呢?
灌满你的水瓶回家去吧。
早晨的时间过去了——沉黑的水不住地流逝。
波浪相互低语嬉笑闲玩着。
流荡的云片聚集在远野高地的天边。
它们留连着悠闲地看着你的脸微笑着。
灌满你的水瓶回家去吧。

Reader

Who are you, reader, reading my poems an hundred years hence?

I cannot send you one single flower from this wealth of the spring, one single streak of gold from yonder clouds.

Open your doors and look abroad.
From your blossoming garden gather fragrant memories of the vanished flowers of an hundred years before.

In the joy of your heart may you feel the living joy that sang one spring morning, sending its glad voice across an hundred years.

读者

你是什么人,读者,百年后读着我的诗?

我不能从春天的财富里送你一朵鲜花,从天边的云彩里送你一片金影。

开起门来四望吧。
从你的群花盛开的园子里,采取百年前消逝了的花儿的芬芳记忆。

在你心的欢乐里,愿你感到一个春晨吟唱的活的欢乐,把它快乐的声音,传过一百年的时间。

吉檀迦利 （冰心 译）

Parting Word

When I go from hence, let this be my parting word, that what I have seen is unsurpassable[1].

I have tasted of the hidden honey of this lotus that expands on the ocean of light, and thus am I blessed—let this be my parting word.

In this playhouse of infinite forms I have had my play and here have I caught sight of him that is formless[2].

My whole body and my limbs have thrilled with his touch who is beyond touch; and if the end comes here, let it come—let this be my parting word.

热词天地

1.unsurpassable ['ʌnsɜ:'pɑ:səbl] *adj.* 无法超越的
2.formless ['fɔ:mləs] *adj.* 没有形状的；无定形的；形体不明的
   from hence 从这里（古英语）
   taste of 体验；有……味道

别话

当我走的时候,让这个作我的别话罢,就是说我所看过的是卓绝无比的。

我曾尝过在光明海上开放的莲花里的隐蜜,因此我受了祝福——让这个作我的别话罢。

在这形象万千的游戏室里,我已经游玩过,在这里我已经瞥见了那无形象的他。

我浑身上下因着那无从接触的他的摩抚而喜颤;假如死亡在这里来临,就让它来好了——让这个作我的别话罢。

Journey

The morning sea of silence broke into ripples of bird songs; and the flowers were all merry by the roadside; and the wealth of gold was scattered through the rift of the clouds while we busily went on our way and paid no heed[1].

We sang no glad songs nor played; we went not to the village for barter; we spoke not a word nor smiled; we lingered not on the way. We quickened our pave more and more as the time sped by.

The sun rose to the mid sky and doves cooed in the shade. Withered[2] leaves danced and whirled in the hot air of noon. The shepherd boy drowsed[3] and dreamed in the shadow of the banyan tree, and I laid myself down by the water and stretched my tired limbs on the grass.

My companions laughed at me in scorn[4]; they held their heads high and hurried on; they never looked back nor rested; they vanished in the distant blue haze. They crossed many meadows and hills, and passed through strange, far-away countries. All honour to you, heroic host of the interminable[5] path! Mockery and reproach pricked me to rise, but found no response in me. I gave myself up for lost in the depth of a glad humiliation—in the shadow of a dim delight.

The repose of the sun-embroidered green gloom slowly spread over

my heart. I forgot for what I had travelled, and I surrendered my mind without struggle to the maze of shadows and songs.

At last, when I woke from my slumber and opened my eyes, I saw thee standing by me, flooding my sleep with thy smile. How I had feared that the path was long and wearisome, and the struggle to reach thee was hard!

热词天地

1. heed. [hi:d] *n.* 注意到；留心到
2. withered ['wɪðəd] *adj.* 枯萎的；憔悴的；雕谢了的
3. drowse [draʊz] *vi.* 打瞌睡；发呆　　*vt.* 使昏昏欲睡；昏昏沉沉地消磨（时光）
4. scorn [skɔ:n] *n.* 轻蔑；嘲笑；藐视的对象
5. interminable [ɪn'tɜ:mɪnəbl] *adj.* 冗长的；无止境的

旅途

清晨的静海,漾起鸟语的微波;路旁的繁花,争妍斗艳;在我们匆忙赶路无心理睬的时候,云隙中散射出灿烂的金光。

我们不唱欢歌,也不嬉游;我们也不到村集中去交易;我们一语不发,也不微笑;我们不在路上留连。时间流逝,我们也加速了脚步。

太阳升到中天,鸽子在凉阴中叫唤。枯叶在正午的炎风中飞舞。牧童在榕树下做他的倦梦,我在水边卧下,在草地上展布我困乏的四肢。

我的同伴们嘲笑我;他们抬头疾走;他们不回顾也不休息;他们消失在远远的碧霭之中。他们穿过许多山林,经过生疏遥远的地方。长途上的英雄队伍呵,光荣是属于你们的!讥笑和责备要促我起立,但我却没有反应。我甘心没落在乐受的耻辱的深处——在模糊的快乐阴影之中。

阳光织成的绿荫的幽静,慢慢的笼罩着我的心。我忘记了旅行的目的,我无抵抗地把我的心灵交给阴影与歌曲的迷宫。

最后,我从沉睡中睁开眼,我看见你站在我身旁,我的睡眠沐浴在你的微笑之中。我从前是如何的惧怕,怕这道路的遥远困难,到你面前的努力是多么艰苦呵!

If the Day Is Done

If the day is done, if birds sing no more, if the wind has flagged tired, then draw the veil of darkness thick upon me, even as thou hast wrapt the earth with the coverlet[1] of sleep and tenderly[2] closed the petals of the drooping lotus at dusk.

From the traveler, whose sack of provisions[3] is empty before the voyage is ended, whose garment is torn and dust-laden, whose strength is exhausted, remove shame and poverty, and renew his life like a flower under the cover of thy kindly night.

热词天地

1.coverlet ['kʌvələt] *n.* 被单；床罩
2.tenderly ['tendəlɪ] *adv.* 温和地；体贴地；柔和地
3.provision [prə'vɪʒn] *n.* 规定；条款；[经] 供应品　*vt.* 供给……食物及必需品
　at dusk 傍晚；黄昏时刻

假如一天已经过去了

假如一天已经过去了,鸟儿也不歌唱,假如风也吹倦了,那就用黑暗的厚幕把我盖上罢,如同你在黄昏时节用睡眠的衾被裹上大地,又轻柔地将睡莲的花瓣合上。

旅客的行程未达,粮袋已空,衣裳破裂污损,而又筋疲力尽,你解除了他的羞涩与困穷,使他的生命像花朵一样在仁慈的夜幕下苏醒。

采果集

Where roads are made I lose my way.

In the wide water, in the blue sky there is no line of a track.

The pathway is hidden by the birds' wings, by the star-fires, by the flowers of the wayfaring[1] seasons.

And I ask my heart if its blood carries the wisdom of the unseen way.

热词天地

1.wayfaring ['weɪˌfeərɪŋ] *adj.* 旅行的 *n.* 徒步旅行

在道路铺成的地方我迷路了。
在无垠的海面上，在蔚蓝的天空下，没有一丝道路的痕迹。
路被飞鸟的羽翼、璀璨的星光、四季流转的繁花遮掩了。
我问自己的心灵，它的血中是否包含着智慧，知晓那条看不见的路。

第四卷 女人如梦

飞鸟集

1

OTroupe[1] of little vagrants[2] of the world, leave your footprints in my words.

热词天地
1.troupe [tru:p] *n.* 剧团，戏班子
2.vagrant ['veɪgrənt] *n.* 流浪者；＜律＞无业游民；乞丐

世间的那群小小的流浪者们啊，
在我的行文舞墨中留下你们的足迹吧！

2

I sit at my window this morning where the world like a passer-by[1] stops for a moment, nods to me and goes.

热词天地

1.passer-by ['pɑːsə baɪ] *n.* 过路人；经过者

整个上午，我静坐窗前，
世界宛如一个行者在那里
停留须臾，向我点点头，便离开。

3

In my solitude of heart I feel the sigh of this widowed[1] evening veiled with mist and rain.

热词天地

1.widowed ['wɪdəʊd] *adj.* 寡居的；鳏居的

这寂寞的黄昏，
沐浴着细雨和薄雾，
我孤伶的心听到了它的哀叹。

4

"In the moon thou sendest thy[1] love letters to me," said the night to the sun.
"I leave my answers in tears upon the grass."

热词天地

1.thy [ðaɪ] *pron.* （旧式用法）你的 (thou 的所有格)

黑夜对太阳说：
"在月色下，你把情书递给了我；
在草地上，我在泪水中回复了你。"

5

Sorrow is hushed into peace in my heart like the evening among the silent trees.

悲伤在我的心里渐渐平静,正如夜晚降临在寂静的树林。

6

Gaps are left in life through which comes the sad music of death.

生命中有着许多罅隙,其间传来死亡的哀伤曲。

7

The night's silence, like a deep lamp,
is burning with the light of its milky way.

夜的静寂,犹如一盏沉默的灯,
银河便是点燃它的火光。

8

My flower of the day dropped its petals[1] forgotten.
In the evening it ripens[2] into a golden fruit of memory.

热词天地

1. petal ['petl] *n.* 花瓣
2. ripen ['raɪpən] *vt.* & *vi.* (使)成熟;(使)熟

我的白昼之花,凋零了它那被忘却的花瓣。
在夜里,它成熟为一粒记忆的金果。

9

The day, with the noise of this little earth, drowns[1] the silence of all worlds.

热词天地

1.drown [draʊn] *vt.* 淹死；浸没

白日，以及这小小地球的喧闹，
掩盖了整个世界的沉默。

10

Leisure[1] in its activity is work.
The stillness of the sea stirs[2] in waves.

热词天地

1.leisure ['leʒə(r)] *n.* 空闲时间；闲暇
2 stir [stɜː(r)] *vt.* & *vi.* （使）移动；搅拌

充满激情的闲暇便是工作。
平静海水的波动便成了潮涌。

11

God comes to me in the dusk[1] of my evening
with the flowers from my past kept fresh in his basket.

热词天地

1.dusk [dʌsk] *n.* 黄昏，傍晚；幽暗

上帝在傍晚的薄暮中，提着花篮向我走来。
这些花都是我记忆里的，它们在花篮里保存得很新鲜。

12

Clouds come floating into my life from other days no longer to shed[1] rain or usher[2] storm but to give colour to my sunset sky.

热词天地

1. shed [ʃed] *vt.* 流出；流下
2. usher [ˈʌʃə(r)] *v.* 引领，招待

从其它时光里飘进我生命里的云彩，不再飘洒雨滴，也不再扬起风雪，却只给与我落日的天空以色彩。

流萤集

1

Migratory songs wing from my heart
and seek their nests in your voice of love.

飘零的歌儿飞出我的心田,
到你爱意盈盈的呼唤中寻找巢窠。

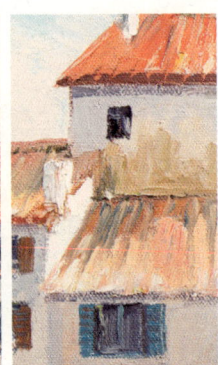

2

The tree is of today, the flower is old,
it brings with it the message
of the immemorial seed.

树木属于今日,花儿却孕育于往昔,
它携来的是关于那古老种子的讯息。

3

In the bounteous time of roses love is wine,—
it is food in the famished hour
when their petals are shed.

在玫瑰盛开的日子里,爱情就是美酒,——
但当落英缤纷的时候,
爱情便成为充饥的食粮。

4

Each rose that comes brings me greetings
from the Rose of an eternal spring.
God honours me when I work,
he loves me when I sing.

每一朵开放的玫瑰都带给我
永恒春天里那朵玫瑰的问候。
当我劳作,神明给我奖赏,
当我歌唱,神明予我爱意。

5

My love of to-day finds no home
in the nest deserted by yesterday's love.

在我昔日之爱遗弃的窝巢里,
我今日的爱找不到栖身之处。

6

The fire of pain traces for my soul
a luminous path across her sorrow.

痛苦的火焰为我的魂灵
照亮了一条穿越哀伤的光明路径。

7

The grass survives the hill
through its resurrections from
countless deaths.

无数次死亡之后的重生，
令小草比山岗更加永恒。

8

An unknown flower in a strange land
speaks to the poet,
"Are we not of the same soil, my lover?"

陌生土地的无名花朵
开口跟诗人搭腔：
"爱人啊，我俩莫不是同乡？"

9

Dawn plays her lute before the gate of darkness,
and is content to vanish when the sun comes out.

黎明对着黑暗之门拔响她的琴弦,
等到太阳出现,便心满意足地消隐。

10

To justify their own spilling of ink they spell the day as night.

为了掩饰自己泼洒的墨水,
他们把白天写成了黑夜。

11

In pity for the desolate branch spring leaves to it a kiss that fluttered in a lonely leaf.

春天对凄凉的孤枝心生怜悯,
于是留给它一个曾在孤叶上飞舞的亲吻。

12

Profit smiles on goodness when the good is profitable.

当好意带来好处时,
好处便对好意微笑。

13

The clouded sky to-day bears the vision
of the shadow of a divine sadness
on the forehead of brooding eternity.

乌云的天空显现出
幽怨的永恒前额那一抹
神圣忧伤的阴影。

14

I am able to love my God
because he gives me freedom to deny him.

我能够爱我的神,
因为他给我拒绝他的自由。

15

My untuned strings beg for music
in their anguished cry of shame.

我那些未曾调律的琴弦
用痛苦而羞惭的叫喊
乞求着音乐。

16

The worm thinks it strange and foolish
that man does not eat his books.

书中的蠹虫认为，
人不以自己的书籍为食，
实在是愚蠢又离奇。

17

Light accepts darkness for his spouse
for the sake of creation.

为了万物的福祉，
光明将黑暗迎娶。

18

The reed waits for his master's breath,
the Master goes seeking for his reed.

芦苇苦苦等待他主人的气息，
主人却在四处寻找自己的芦苇。

19

To the blind pen the hand that writes is unreal,
its writing unmeaning.

盲目的笔认为
那写作的手并不真实，
它所写的字也全无意义。

20

The sea smites his own barren breast
because he has no flowers to offer to
the moon.

大海捶打自己光秃秃的胸膛，
因为他没有花朵来献给月亮。

园丁集 （冰心译）

Where Do You Hurry?

Where do you hurry with your basket this late evening when the marketing is over?

They all have come home with their burdens; the moon peeps from above the village trees.

The echoes of the voices calling for the ferry run across the dark water to the distant swamp where wild ducks sleep.

Where do you hurry with your basket when the marketing is over?

Sleep has laid her fingers upon the eyes of the earth.

The nests of the crows have become silent, and the murmurs of the bamboo leaves are silent.

The labourers home from their fields spread their mats in the courtyards.

Where do you hurry with your basket when the marketing is over?

你急忙地要到哪里去呢？

集市已过，你在夜晚急急地提着篮子要到哪里去呢？
他们都挑着担子回家去了；月亮从村树隙中下窥。

唤船的回声从深黑的水上传到远处野鸭睡眠的泽沼。

在市集已过的时候，你提着篮子急忙地要到哪里去呢？

睡眠把她的手指按在大地的双眼上。
鸦巢已静，竹叶的微语也已沉默。

劳动的人们从田间归来，把席子展铺在院子里。
在市集已过的时候，你提着篮子急忙地要到哪里去呢？

It Is Evening

I try to weave a wreath all the morning, but the flowers slip and they drop out.

You sit there watching me in secret through the corner of your prying eyes.

Ask those eyes, darkly planning mischief, whose fault it was.

I try to sing a song, but in vain.

A hidden smile trembles on your lips, ask of it the reason of my failure.

Let your smiling lips say on oath how my voice lost itself in silence like a drunken bee in the lotus.

It is evening, and the time for the flowers to close their petals.

Give me how to sit by your side, and bid my lips to do the work that can be done in silence and in dim light of stars.

夜晚了

整个早晨我想编一个花环,但是花儿滑掉了。
你坐在一旁偷偷地从侦伺的眼角看着我。
问这一对沉黑的恶作剧的眼睛,这是谁的错。

我想唱一支歌,但是唱不出来。
一个暗笑在你唇上颤动;你问它我失败的缘由。
让你微笑的唇儿发一个誓,说我的歌声怎样地消失在沉默里,像一只在荷花里沉醉的蜜蜂。

夜晚了,是花瓣合起的时候了。
容许我坐在你的旁边,容许我的唇儿做那在沉默中、在星辰的微光中能做的工作吧。

When I Come Again

An unbelieving smile flits on your eyes when I come to you to take my leave.
I have done it so often that you think I will soon return.

To tell you the truth I have the same doubt in my mind.
For the spring days come again time after time, the full moon takes leave and comes on another visit, the flower come again and blush upon their branches year after year, and it is likely that I take my leave only to come to you again.

But keep the illusion awhile; do not send it away with ungentle haste.
When I say I leave you for all time, accept it as true, and let a mist of tears for one moment deepen the dark rim of your eyes.

Then smile as archly as you like when I come again.

当我再来的时候

一个怀疑的微笑在你眼中闪烁,当我来向你告别的时候。
我这样做的次数太多了,你想我很快又会回来。

告诉你实话,我自己心里也有同样的怀疑。
因为春天年年回来,满月道过别又来访问,花儿每年回来在枝上红晕着脸,很可能我向你告别只为的要再回到你的身边。

但是把这幻象保留一会吧,不要冷酷粗率地把它赶走。
当我说我要永远离开你的时候,就当作真话来接受它,让泪雾暂时加深你眼边的黑影。

当我再来的时候,随便你怎样地狡笑吧。

A Woman Is Like a Dream

O woman, you are not merely the handiwork of God, but also of men; these are ever endowing you with beauty from their hearts.

Poets are weaving for you a web with threads of golden imagery; painters are giving your form ever new immortality.

The sea gives its pearls, the mines their gold, the summer gardens their flowers to deck you, to cover you, to make you more precious.

The desire of men's hearts has shed its glory over your youth.

You are one half woman and one half dream.

女人如梦

啊,女人,你不但是神的,而且是人的手工艺品;他们永远从心里用美来打扮你。

诗人们用比喻的金线替你织网,画家们给你的身形以永新的不朽。
海献上珍珠,矿献上金子,夏日的花园献上花朵来装扮你,覆盖你,使你更加美妙。

人类心中的愿望,在你的青春上洒上光荣……
你一半是女人,一半是梦。

I Dare Not

I long to speak the deepest words I have to say to you; but I dare not, for fear you should laugh.

That is why I laugh at myself and shatter my secret in jest.

I make light of my pain, afraid you should do so.

I long to tell you the truest words I have to say you; but I dare not, being afraid that you would not believe them.

That is why I disguise them in untruth, saying the contrary of what I mean.

I make my pain appear absurd, afraid that you should do so.

I long to use the most precious words I have for you; but I dare not, fearing I should not be paid with like value.

That is why I give you hard names and boast of my callous strength.
I hurt you, for fear you would never know any pain.

I long to sit silent by you; but I dare not lest my heart come out at my lips.
That is why I prattle and chatter lightly and hide my heart behind words.
I rudely handle my pain, for fear you should do so.

I long to go away from your side; but I dare not, for fear my cowardice should become known to you.
That is why I hold my head high and carelessly come into your presence.
Constant thrusts from your eyes keep my pain fresh for ever.

我不敢

我想对你说出我要说的最深的话语,我不敢,我怕你哂笑。
因此我嘲笑自己,把我的秘密在玩笑中打碎。
我把我的痛苦说得轻松,因为怕你会这样做。

我想对你说出我要说的最真的话语,我不敢,我怕你不信。
因此我弄真成假,说出和我的真心相反的话。
我把我的痛苦说得可笑,因为我怕你会这样做。

我想用最宝贵的名词来形容你,我不敢,我怕得不到相当的酬报。
因此我给你安上苛刻的名字,而夸示我的硬骨。
我伤害你,因为怕你永远不知道我的痛苦。

我渴望静默地坐在你的身旁,我不敢,怕我的心会跳到我的唇上。
因此我轻松地说东道西,把我的心藏在语言的后面。
我粗暴地对待我的痛苦,因为我怕你会这样做。

我渴望从你身边走开,我不敢,怕你看出我的懦怯。
因此我随随便便地昂着头走到你的面前。
从你眼里频频掷来的刺激,使我的痛苦永远新鲜。

Drunk, I Will Follow You

O mad, superbly drunk;
If you kick open your doors and play the fool in public;
If you empty your bag in a night, and snap your fingers at prudence;
If you walk in curious paths and play with useless things;
Reck not rhyme or reason;
If unfurling your sails before the storm you snap the rudder in two,
Then I will follow you, comrade, and be drunken and go to the dogs.

I have wasted my days and nights in the company of steady wise neighbors.

Much knowing has turned my hair grey, and much watching has made my sight dim.

For years I have gathered and heaped up scraps and fragments of them:

Crush them and dance upon them, and scatter them all to the winds.

For I know 'tis the height of wisdom to be drunken and go to the dogs.

Let all crooked scruples vanish, let me hopelessly lose my way.

Let a gust of wild giddiness come and sweep me away from my anchors.

The world is peopled with worthies, and workers, useful and clever.

There are men who are easily first, and men who come decently after.

Let them be happy and prosper, and let me be foolishly futile.

For I know 'tis the end of all works to be drunken and go to the dogs.

I swear to surrender this moment all claims to the ranks of the decent.

I let go my pride of learning and judgment of right and of wrong.

I'll shatter memory's vessel, scattering the last the drop of tears.

With the foam of the berry-red wine I will bathe and brighten my laughter.

The badge of the civil and staid I'll tear into shreds for the nonce.

I'll take the holy vow to be worthless, to be drunken and go to the dogs.

醉汉,我要跟随你

呵,疯狂的、头号的醉汉;
如果你踢开门户在大众面前装疯;
如果你在一夜倒空囊橐,对慎重轻蔑地弹着指头;
如果你走着奇怪的道路,和无益的东西游戏;
不理会韵律和理性;
如果你在风暴前扯起船帆,你把船舵折成两半,
那么我就要跟随你,伙伴,喝得烂醉走向堕落灭亡。

我在稳重聪明的街坊中间虚度了日日夜夜。
过多的知识使我白了头发,过多的观察使我眼力模糊。
多年来我积攒了许多零碎的东西;
把这些东西摔碎,在上面跳舞,把它们散掷到风中去吧。

因为我知道喝得烂醉而堕落灭亡,是最高的智慧。

让一切歪曲的顾虑消亡吧,让我无望地迷失了路途。
让一阵旋风吹来,把我连船锚一齐卷走。

世界上住着高尚的人,劳动的人,有用又聪明。
有的人很从容地走在前头,有的人庄重地走在后面。
让他们快乐繁荣吧,让我傻呆地无用吧。
因为我知道喝得烂醉而堕落灭亡,是一切工作的结局。

我此刻誓将一切的要求,让给正人君子。
我抛弃我学识的自豪和是非的判断。
我打碎记忆的瓶壶,挥洒最后的眼泪。
以红果酒的泡沫来洗澡,使我欢笑发出光辉。
我暂且撕裂温恭和认真的标志。
我将发誓作一个无用的人,喝得烂醉而堕落灭亡下去。

Forgive This Pair of Sinners

Reverend sir, forgive this pair of sinners.
Spring winds to-day are blowing in wild eddies, driving dust and dead leaves away, and with them your lessons are all lost.

Do not say, father, that life is a vanity.

For me have made truce with death for once, and only for a few fragrant hours we two have been made immortal.

Even if the king's army came and fiercely fell upon us we should sadly shake our heads and say, brothers, you are disturbing us. If you must have this noisy game, go and clatter your arms elsewhere.

Since only for a few fleeting moments we have been made immortal.

If friendly people came and flocked around us, we should humbly bow to them and say, this extravagant good fortune is an embarrassment to us. Room is scare in the infinite sky where we dwell. For in the springtime flowers come in crowds, and the busy wings of bees jostle each other. Our little heaven, where dwell only we two immortals, is too absurdly narrow.

饶恕这一对罪人吧

尊敬的长者,饶恕这一对罪人吧。

今天春风猖狂地吹起旋舞,把尘土和枯叶都扫走了,你的功课也随着一起丢掉了。

师父,不要说生命是虚空的。

因为我们和死亡订下一次和约,在一段温馨的时间中,我俩变成不朽。

即使是国王的军队凶猛地前来追捕,我们将忧愁地摇头说,弟兄们,你们扰乱了我们了。如果你们必须做这个吵闹的游戏,到别处去敲击你们的武器吧。

因为我们刚在这片刻飞逝的时光中变成不朽。

如果亲切的人们来把我们围起,我们将恭敬地向他们鞠躬说,这个荣幸使我们惭愧。在我们居住的无限天空之中,没有多少隙地。因为在春天繁花盛开,蜜蜂的忙碌的翅翼也彼此摩挤。只住着我们两个仙人的小天堂,是狭小得太可笑了。

Time Is Short

You left me and went on your way.

I thought I should mourn for you and set your solitary image in my heart wrought in a golden song.

But ah, my evil fortune, time is short.

Youth wanes year after year; the spring days are fugitive; the frail flowers die for nothing, and the wise man warns me that life is but a dewdrop on the lotus leaf.

Should I neglect all this to gaze after one who has turned her back on me?

That should be rude and foolish, for time is short.

Then, come, my rainy nights with pattering feet; smile, my golden autumn; come, careless April, scattering your kisses abroad.

You come, and you, and you also!

My loves, you know we are mortals. Is it wise to break one's heart for the one who takes her heart away? For time is short.

It is sweet to sit in a corner to muse and write in rhymes that you are all my world.

It is heroic to hug one's sorrow and determine not to be consoled.

But a fresh face peeps across my door and raises its eyes to my eyes.

I cannot but wipe away my tears and change the tune of my song.

For time is short.

时间是短暂的

你离开我自己走了。

我想我将为你忧伤,还将用金色的诗歌铸成你孤寂的形象,供养在我的心里。

但是,我的运气多坏,时间是短促的。

青春一年一年地消逝;春日是暂时的;柔弱的花朵无意义地调谢,聪明人警告我说,生命只是一颗荷叶上的露珠。

我可以不管这些,只凝望着背弃我的那个人么?

这会是无益的,愚蠢的,因为时间是太短暂了。

那么,来吧,我的雨夜的脚步声;微笑吧,我的金色的秋天;来吧,无虑无忧的四月,散掷着你的亲吻。

你来吧,还有你,也有你!

我的情人们,你知道我们都是凡人。为一个取回她的心的人而心碎,是件聪明的事情么?因为时间是短暂的。

坐在屋角凝思,把我的世界中的你们都写在韵律里,是甜柔的。

把自己的忧伤抱紧,决不受人安慰,是英勇的。

但是一个新的面庞,在我门外偷窥,抬起眼来看我的眼睛。

我只能拭去眼泪,更改我歌曲的腔调。

因为时间是短暂的。

If

If you would have it so, I will end my singing.

If it sets your heart aflutter, I will take away my eyes from your face.

If it suddenly startles you in your walk, I will step aside and take another path.

If it confuses you in your flower-weaving, I will shun your lonely garden.

If it makes the water wanton and wild, I will not row my boat by your bank.

如果

如果你要这样,我就停了歌唱。
如果它使你心震颤,我就把眼光从你脸上挪开。
如果它使你在行走时忽然惊跃,我就躲开另走别路。

如果它在你编串花环时使你烦乱,我就避开你寂寞的花园。
如果它使水花飞溅,我就不在你的河边划船。

Why Did You Single Me Out

I was one among many women busy with the obscure daily tasks of the household.

Why did you single me out and bring me away from the cool shelter of our common life?

Love unexpressed is sacred. It shines like gems in the gloom of the hidden heart. In the light of the curious day it looks pitifully dark.

Ah, you broke through the cover of my heart and dragged my trembling love into the open place, destroying for ever the shady corner where it hid its nest.

The other women are the same as ever.

No one has peeped into their inmost being, and they themselves know not their own secret.

Lightly they smile, and weep, chatter, and work. Daily they go to the temple, light their lamps, and fetch water from the river.

I hope my love would be saved from the shivering shame of the shelterless, but you turn your face away.

Yes, your path lies open before you, but you have cut off my return, and left me stripped naked before the world with its lidless eyes staring night and day.

你为什么把我挑选出来

我是妇女中为平庸的日常家务而忙碌的一个。
你为什么把我挑选出来,把我从日常生活的凉荫中带出来?

没有表现出来的爱是神圣的。它像宝石般在隐藏的心的朦胧里放光。在奇异的日光中,它显得可怜地晦暗。
呵,你打碎我心的盖子,把我颤栗的爱情拖到空旷的地方,把那阴暗的藏我心巢的一角永远破坏了。

别的女人和从前一样。
没有一个人窥探到自己的最深处,她们不知道自己的秘密。
她们轻快地微笑,哭泣,谈话,工作。她们每天到庙里去,点上她们的灯,还到河中取水。

我希望能从无遮拦的颤羞中把我的爱情救出,但是你掉头不顾。
是的,你的前途是远大的,但是你把我的归路切断了,让我在世界的无睫毛的眼睛日夜瞪视之下赤裸着。

Free Me from Your Bonds

Free me from the bonds of your sweetness, my love! No more of this wine of kisses.
This mist of heavy incense stifles my heart.
Open the doors, make room for the morning light.

I am lost in you, wrapped in the folds of your caresses.
Free me from your spells, and give me back the manhood to offer you my freed heart.

把我从你的枷锁中放出来吧

把我从你甜柔的枷锁中放出来吧,我爱,不要再斟上亲吻的酒。
香烟的浓雾窒塞了我的心。
开起门来,让晨光进入吧!

我消失在你里面,包缠在你爱抚的折痕之中。
把我从你的诱惑中放出来吧,把男子气概交还我,好让我把得到自由的心贡献给你。

The Gardener

It was mid-day when you went away.
The sun was strong in the sky.
I had done my work and sat alone on my balcony when you went away.
Fitful gusts came winnowing[1] through the smells of many distant fields.

The doves cooed tireless in the shade, and a bee strayed in my room humming the news of many distant fields.
The village slept in the noonday heat. The road lay deserted.
In sudden fits the rustling of the leaves rose and died.

I glazed at the sky and wove in the blue the letters of a name I had known, while the village slept in the noonday heat.

I had forgotten to braid my hair. The languid² breeze played with it upon my cheek.

The river ran unruffled³ under the shady bank.

The lazy white clouds did not move.

I had forgotten to braid my hair.

It was mid-day when you went away.

The dust of the road was hot and the fields panting⁴.

The doves cooed among the dense leaves.

I was alone in my balcony when you went away.

热词天地

1. winnow ['wɪnəʊ] *v.* 扬；辨别；选择；除去
2. languid ['læŋgwɪd] *adj.* 倦怠的；呆滞的；软弱无力的
3. unruffled [ʌn'rʌfld] *adj.* 平静的；不骚动的；镇定的
4. panting ['pæntɪŋ] *adj.* 喘气的

   go away 离开

园丁

正午的时候你走了。
烈日当空。
当你走的时候,我已做完了工作,坐在凉台上。
不定的风吹来,含带着许多远野的香气。

鸽子在树荫中不停地叫唤,一只蜜蜂在我屋里飞着,嗡出许多远野的消息。
村庄在午热中入睡了。路上无人。
树叶的声音时起时息。

我凝望天空,把一个我知道的名字织在蔚蓝里。当村庄在午热中入睡的时候。

我忘记把头发编起。困倦的风在我颊上和它嬉戏。
河水在荫岸下平静地流动。
懒散的白云动也不动。
我忘了编起我的头发。

正午的时候你走了。
路上尘土灼热,田野在喘息。
鸽子在密叶中呼唤。
我独坐在凉台上,当你走的时候。

吉檀迦利 （冰心 译）

Tired Eyes

In the night of weariness let me give myself up to sleep without struggle, resting my trust upon thee.

Let me not force my flagging[1] spirit into a poor preparation[2] for thy worship.

It is thou who drawest the veil of night upon the tired eyes of the day to renew its sight in a fresher gladness of awakening.

热词天地
1.flagging ['flægɪŋ] *adj.* 下垂的；衰弱的
2.preparation [ˌprepə'reɪʃn] *n.* 预备；准备

倦眼

在这困倦的夜里，让我帖服地把自己交给睡眠，把信赖托付给你。

让我不去勉强我的萎靡的精神，来准备一个对你敷衍的礼拜。

是你拉上夜幕盖上白日的倦眼，使这眼神在醒觉的清新喜悦中，更新了起来。

新月集

The Flower-School

When storm clouds rumble[1] in the sky and June showers come down, the moist east wind comes marching over the heath to blow its bagpipes among the bamboos.

Then crowds of flowers come out of a sudden, from nobody knows where, and dance upon the grass in wild glee[2].

Mother, I really think the flowers go to school underground.

They do their lessons with doors shut, and if they want to come out to play before it is time, their master makes them stand in a corner.

When the rains come they have their holidays.

Branches clash together in the forest, and the leaves rustle in the wild wind. The thunder-clouds clap their giant hands and the flower children rush out in dresses of pink and yellow and white.

Do you know, mother, their home is in the sky, where the stars are.

Haven't you seen how eager they are to get there? Don't you know why they are in such a hurry?

Of course, I can guess to whom they raise their arms: they have their mother as I have my own.

热词天地

1.rumble ['rʌmbl] vi. 隆隆作响 vt. 低沉地说 n. 隆隆声，辘辘声
2.glee [gli:] n. 快乐，欢喜

花的学校

当雷云在天上轰鸣,六月的阵雨落下的时候,润湿的东风掠过荒野,在竹林中吹起口笛。

于是花从无人知道的地方,突然一群一群地跑出来,在绿草地上跳着舞,狂欢着。

妈妈,我真的觉得那群花朵是在地下的学校里上学。

他们关了门做功课,如果他们想在散学以前出来做游戏,他们的老师是要责罚他们站壁角的。

雨一来,他们便放假了。

树枝在林中互相触碰着,绿叶在狂风里飒飒作响。雷云拍起了大手,花孩子们便在那时候穿了紫的、黄的、白的衣裳,冲了出来。

你可知道,妈妈,他们的家是在天上,是那星星所住的地方。

你没有看见他们怎样地渴望着要到那儿去吗?你不知道他们为什么那样急切吗?

我自然能够猜得出他们是对谁扬起手臂来:他们也有他们的妈妈,就像我有我自己的妈妈一样。

第五卷 地牢

飞鸟集

1

I thank thee that I am none of the wheels of power but I am one with the living creatures that are crushed[1] by it.

热词天地

1. crush [krʌʃ] vt. 压破，压碎；镇压

感谢上帝，我不是权力的任一车轮，
而是被其碾压的一个生命。

2

Man does not reveal[1] himself in his history, he struggles[2] up through it.

热词天地
1. reveal [rɪ'viːl] *vt.* 显露；揭露
2. struggle ['strʌgl] *vi.* 搏斗；奋斗；努力

人类并没有在历史中表现自我，
而只是在其中峥嵘前行。

3

What you are you do not see, what you see is your shadow[1].

热词天地

1.shadow [ˈʃædəʊ] *n.* 阴影；影子

你并非看到了真实的自我，
你所看到的只是自己的影子。

4

God finds himself by creating.

上帝在创造中找到了他自己。

5

Man barricades[1] against himself.

热词天地

1. barricade [ˌbærɪ'keɪd] *vt.* 设路障于，以障碍物阻塞；封锁，阻挡

人们常常给自己设障重重。

6

The scabbard[1] is content to be dull when it protects the keenness[2] of the sword.

热词天地

1. scabbard ['skæbəd] *n.* （剑）鞘，套
2. keenness ['ki:nnɪs] *n.* 敏锐

剑鞘在保护剑的锋利时，
满足于自己的驽钝。

7

God is ashamed when the prosperous[1] boasts of His special favour.

热词天地

1. prosperous ['prɒspərəs] *adj.* 繁荣的，兴旺的；富裕的
   boast of 夸耀，吹嘘；夸示

当富人吹嘘他们得到了上帝的特惠时，
上帝却感到羞愧了。

8

Praise shames me, for I secretly beg for it.

热词天地
beg for 乞讨（食物、钱等）

荣耀让我感到惭愧，因为我曾偷偷地乞求过它。

9

I have dipped[1] the vessel[2] of my heart into this silent hour;
it has filled with love.

热词天地
1.dip [dɪp] *vt.* 浸
2.vessel ['vesl] *n.* 容器

我将心之钵沉浸在这寂静时刻，
它已盛满了爱。

10

I live in this little world of mine
and am afraid to make it the least less.
Lift me into thy world
and let me have the freedom gladly to lose my all.

我住在我的小小世界中,
生怕它变得更小。
请把我带去您的世界吧,
让我自由地失去我的所有。

11

My heart has spread its sails to the idle[1] winds for the shadowy island of anywhere.

热词天地

1.idle ['aɪdl] *adj.* 无意义的；空闲的

我的心顺着阑珊的风儿张开了帆，
只为到达任意的荫凉之岛。

12

Let my doing nothing when I have nothing to do
become untroubled in its depth of peace
like the evening in the seashore when the water
is silent.

当我百无聊赖时,让我什么也别做,
免于纷扰地沉入平静的深处吧,
一如波涛平静时的海滨夜色。

13

Timid thoughts, do not be afraid of me.
I am a poet.

热词天地

be afraid of 害怕，担忧

腼腆的思想啊，别怕我。
我只是一个诗人。

14

My heart is homesick[1] today
for the one sweet hour across the sea of time.

热词天地

1.homesick ['həʊmsɪk] *adj.* 想家的；患思乡病的

今天，我很想家，
为了那流逝岁月中的温馨一刻。

15

Let me live truly, my Lord[1], so that death to me become true.

热词天地

1.lord [lo:d] *n.* 主；领主；上帝

　　让我实实在在地生活吧，主啊。这样，死亡对我而言就变成真实了。

16

Man's history is waiting in patience[1] for the triumph[2] of the insulted man.

热词天地

1.patience ['peɪʃns] *n.* 耐心；耐性
2.triumph ['traɪʌmf] *n.* 胜利；巨大的成就

　　人类的历史就是在忍耐中
等待着受辱者的胜利。

流萤集

1

The tree bears its thousand years
as one large majestic moment.

大树将自己走过的万载千年，
呈现为一个壮丽而庄严的瞬间。

2

Your smile, my love, like the smell of a strange flower,
is simple and inexplicable.

我的爱人啊，你的笑靥，就像那奇异花朵的芳馨，
简单素朴，无从索解。

3

The sigh of the shore follows in vain the breeze that hastens the ship across the sea.

海岸的叹息，徒然地追踪着
吹送船儿过海的轻风。

4

The right to possess boasts foolishly of its right to enjoy.

占有的权利总是愚蠢地夸说
它享受的权利。

5

The rose is a great deal more
than a blushing apology for the thorn.

玫瑰的意义远不只是
因棘刺而生的一份赧然歉意。

6

Day offers to the silence of stars
his golden lute to be tuned
for the endless life.

为了永恒的生命,
白昼将自己的金琴交给
静谧的繁星去调谐。

7

The wise know how to teach,
the fool how to smite.

智者懂得如何教化,
愚者只知如何责罚。

8

The judge thinks that he is just when he compares
the oil of another's lamp
with the light of his own.

裁判者将他人的灯油
与自己的灯光相比,
自认为他公平合理。

9

The spirit of work in creation is there to carry and help the spirit of play.

造物之所以有劳作的热情，
只是为了助长游戏的兴致。

10

Faith is the bird that feels the light and sings when the dawn is still dark.

信念是能感知光明的小鸟，
在未明的破晓啁啾歌唱。

11

I bring to thee, night, my day's empty cup
to be cleansed with thy cool darkness
for a new morning's festival.

夜啊,我为你带来白昼之空杯,
请你用清凉的黑暗将它净洗,
好迎接崭新清晨的欢庆。

12

Leaves are silences
around flowers which are their words.

叶儿是环绕花儿的静默,
花儿是叶儿的语言。

13

The mountain fir, in its rustling,
modulates the memory of its fights with the storm
into a hymn of peace.

飒飒作响的峰顶冷杉,
将抗击风暴的往事
协奏为赞美和平的颂诗。

14

The captive flower in the King's wreath smiles bitterly when the meadow-flower envies her.

面对草地上野花的羡慕,
囚在国王花冠里的花儿笑得悲苦。

15

Its store of snow is the hill's own burden, its outpouring of streams is borne by all the world.

积雪的重负由山岳自己承揽,
融流的溪水却由整个世界来分享。

园丁集 （冰心译）

I Forget

I am restless. I am athirst[1] for far-away things.
My soul goes out in a longing to touch the skirt of the dim[2] distance.
O Great Beyond, O the keen call of thy flute!
I forget, I ever forget, that I have no wings to fly, that I am bound in this spot evermore.

I am eager[3] and wakeful, I am a stranger in a strange land.
Thy breath comes to me whispering an impossible hope.
Thy tongue is known to my heart as its very own.
O Far-to-seek, O the keen call of thy flute!
I forget, I ever forget, that I know not the way, that I have not the winged horse.

I am listless, I am a wanderer in my heart.

In the sunny haze[4] of the languid hours, what vast vision of thine takes shape in the blue of the sky!

O Farthest end, O the keen call of thy flute!

I forget, I ever forget, that the gates are shut everywhere in the house where I dwell alone!

热词天地

1.athirst [əˈθɜːst] *adj.* 渴望的；口渴的
2.dim [dɪm] *adj.* 暗淡的，昏暗的
3.eager [ˈiːgə(r)] *adj.* 渴望的；热切的
4.haze [heɪz] *n.* 烟雾；迷蒙
　be known to 为……所熟知
　take shape in 具体化，成形，体现

我忘却了

我心绪不宁。我渴望着遥远的事物。
我的灵魂在极想中走出,要去摸触幽暗的远处的边缘。
呵,"伟大的来生",呵,你笛声的高亢的呼唤!
我忘却了,我总是忘却了,我没有奋飞的翅翼,我永远在这地点系住。

我切望而又清醒,我是一个异乡的异客。
你的气息向我低语出一个不可能的希望。
我的心懂得你的语言,就像它懂得自己的语言一样。
呵,"遥远的寻求",呵,你笛声的高亢的呼唤!
我忘却了,我总是忘却了,我不认得路,我也没有生翼的马。

我心绪不宁。我是自己心中的流浪者。
在疲倦时光的日霭中,你广大的幻象在天空的蔚蓝中显现!
呵,"最远的尽头",呵,你笛声的高亢的呼唤!
我忘却了,我总是忘却了,在我独居的房子里,所有的门户都是紧闭的!

I Know Not What You Thought of Me

Why do you put me to shame with a look?
I have not come as a beggar[1].

Only for a passing hour I stood at the end of your courtyard outside the garden hedge.

Why do you put me to shame with a look?

Not a rose did I gather from your garden, not a fruit did I pluck[2].

I humbly took my shelter under the wayside shade where every strange traveller may stand.

Not a rose did I pluck.

Yes, my feet were tired, and the shower of rain come down.

The winds cried out among the swaying bamboo branches.

The clouds ran across the sky as though in the flight from defeat.

My feet were tired.

I know not what you thought of me or for whom you were waiting at your door.

Flashes of lightning dazzled[3] your watching eyes.

How could I know that you could see me where I stood in the dark?

I know not what you thought of me.

The day is ended, and the rain has ceased for a moment.

I leave the shadow of the tree at the end of your garden and this seat on the grass.

It has darkened; shut your door; I go my way.

The day is ended.

热词天地

1. beggar ['begə(r)] *n.* 乞丐；家伙
2. pluck [plʌk] *vt.* 采，摘；拔掉
3. dazzle ['dæzl] *vt.* 使目眩；使惊异不已
   put sb. to shame 羞辱某人
   for a moment 片刻，一会儿；霎时之间

我不知道你怎样看待我

为什么你盯着我使我羞愧呢?
我不是来求乞的。
只为要消磨时光,我才来站在你院边的篱外。
为什么你盯着我使我羞愧呢?

我没有从你园里采走一朵玫瑰,没有摘下一颗果子。
我谦卑地在任何生客都可站立的路边棚下找个荫蔽。
我没有采走一朵玫瑰。

是的,我的脚疲乏了,骤雨又落了下来。
风在摇曳的竹林中呼叫。
云阵像败退似的跑过天空。
我的脚疲乏了。

我不知道你怎样看待我,或是你在门口等什么人。
闪电昏眩了你看望的目光。
我怎能知道你会看到站在黑暗中的我呢?
我不知道你怎样看待我。

白日过尽,雨势暂停。
我离开你园畔的树阴和草地上的座位。
日光已暗;关上你的门户吧;我走我的路。
白日过尽了。

Beauty, Carved in Stone

Amidst the rush and roar of life, O Beauty, carved in stone, you stand mute and still, alone and aloof.

Great Time sits enamoured at your feet and murmurs:
"Speak, speak to me, my love; speak, my bride!"

But your speech is shut up in stone, O Immovable Beauty!

石头雕成的"美"

在生命奔腾怒吼的中流,啊,石头雕成的"美",你冷静无言,独自超绝地站立着。

"伟大的时间"依恋地坐在你脚边低语说:
"说话吧,对我说话吧,我爱;说话吧,我的新娘!"

但是你的话被石头关住了,啊,不动的美!

My Heart Longs for the Meeting with You

Love, my heart longs day and night for the meeting with you—for the meeting that is like all-devouring death.

Sweep me away like a storm; take everything I have; break open my sleep and plunder my dreams. Rob me of my world.

In that devastation, in the utter nakedness of spirit, let us become one in beauty.

Alas for my vain desire! Where is this hope for union except in thee, my God?

我的心想望和你相见

爱,我的心日夜想望和你相见——那像吞灭一切的死亡一样的会见。

像一阵风暴把我卷走;把我的一切都拿去;劈开我的睡眠抢走我的梦。剥夺了我的世界。

在这毁灭里,在精神的全部赤露里,让我们在美中合一吧。

我的空想是可怜的!除了在你里面,哪有这合一的希望呢,我的神?

I Have Not My Rose

I plucked your flower, O world!
I pressed it to my heart and the thorn pricked.
When the day waned and it darkened, I found that the flower had faded, but the pain remained.

More flowers will come to you with perfume and pride, O world!
But my time for flower-gathering is over, and through the dark night I have not my rose, only the pain remains.

我没有了玫瑰

我采了你的花,呵,世界!
我把它压在胸前,花刺伤了我。
日光渐暗,我发现花儿凋谢了,痛苦却存留着。

许多有香有色的花又将来到你这里,呵,世界!
但是我采花的时代过去了,黑夜悠悠,我没有了玫瑰,只有痛苦存留着。

Here Is the Same Sky

She dwelt on the hillside by the edge of a maize-field, near the spring that flows in laughing rills through the solemn shadows of ancient trees. The women came there to fill their jars, and travellers would sit there to rest and talk. She worked and dreamed daily to the tune of the bubbling stream.

One evening the stranger came down from the cloud-hidden peak; his locks were tangled like drowsy snakes. We asked in wonder, "Who are you?" He answered not but sat by the garrulous stream and silently gazed at the hut where she dwelt. Our hearts quaked in fear and we came back home when it was night.

Next morning when the women came to fetch water at the spring by the deodar trees, they found the doors open in her hut, but her voice was gone and where was her smiling face? The empty jar lay on the floor and her lamp had burnt itself out in the corner. No one knew where she had fled to before it was morning—and the stranger had gone.

In the month of May the sun grew strong and the snow melted, and we sat by the spring and wept. We wondered in our mind, "Is there a spring in the land where she has gone and where she can fill her vessel in these hot thirsty days?" And we asked each other in dismay, "Is there a land beyond these hills where we live?"

It was a summer night; the breeze blew from the south; and I sat in her deserted room where the lamp stood still unlit. When suddenly from before my eyes the hills vanished like curtains drawn aside. "Ah, it is she who comes. How are you, my child? Are you happy? But where can you shelter under this open sky? And, alas, our spring is not here to allay your thirst."

"Here is the same sky," she said, "only free from the fencing hills, —this is the same stream grown into a plain." "Everything is here," I sighed, "only we are not." She smiled sadly and said, "You are in my heart." I woke up and heard the babbling of the stream and the rustling of the deodars at night.

那边还是那个天空

她住在玉米地边的山畔,靠近那股嬉笑着流经古树的庄严的阴影的清泉。女人们提罐到这里来装水,过客们在这里谈话休息。她每天随着潺潺的泉韵工作幻想。

有一天傍晚,一个陌生人从云中的山上下来;他的头发像醉蛇一样的纷乱。我们惊奇地问,"你是谁?"他不回答,只坐在喧闹的水边沉默地望着她的茅屋。我们吓得心跳。到了夜里我们都回家去了。

第二天早晨,女人们到杉树下的泉边取水,她们发现她茅屋的门开着,但是,她的声音没有了,她的微笑的脸哪里去了呢?空罐立在地上,她屋角的灯,油尽火灭了。没有人晓得在黎明以前,她跑到哪里去了——那个陌生人也不见了。

到了五月,阳光渐强,冰雪化尽,我们坐在泉边哭泣。我们心里想,"她去的地方有泉水么,在这炎热焦渴的天气中,她能到哪里去取水呢?"我们惶恐地对问,"在我们住的山外还有地方么?"

夏天的夜里,微风从南方吹来;我坐在她的空屋里,没有点上的灯仍在那里立着。忽然间那座山峰,像帘幕拉开一样从我眼前消失了。"呵,那是她来了。你好么,我的孩子?你快乐么?在无遮的天空下,你有个荫凉的地方么?可怜呵,我们的泉水不在这里供你解渴。"

"那边还是那个天空,"她说,"只是不受屏山的遮隔,——也还是那股流泉长成江河,——也还是那片土地伸广变成平原。""一切都有了,"我叹息说,"只有我们不在。"她含愁地笑着说:"你们是在我的心里。"我醒起听见泉流潺潺,杉树的叶子在夜中沙沙地响着。

My Bride and I

We are to play the game of death to-night, my bride and I. The night is black, the clouds in the sky are capricious, and the waves are raving at sea.

We have left our bed of dreams, flung open the door and come out, my bride and I.

We sit upon a swing, and the storm winds give us a wild push from behind.

My bride starts up with fear and delight, she trembles and clings to my breast.

Long have I served her tenderly.

I made for her a bed of flowers and I closed the doors to shut out the rude light from her eyes.

I kissed her gently on her lips and whispered softly in her ears till she half swooned in languor.

She was lost in the endless mist of vague sweetness.

She answered not to my touch, my songs failed to arouse her.

To-night has come to us the call of the storm from the wild.

My bride has shivered and stood up, she has clasped my hand and come out.

Her hair is flying in the wind, her veil is fluttering, her garland rustles over her breast.

The push of death has swung her into life.

We are face to face and heart to heart, my bride and I.

我的新娘和我

我们今夜要做"死亡"的游戏,我的新娘和我。
夜是深黑的,空中的云霾是翻腾的,波涛在海里泡哮。

我们离开梦的床榻,推门出去,我的新娘和我。
我们坐在秋千上,狂风从后面猛烈地推送我们。
我的新娘吓得又惊又喜,她颤抖着紧靠在我的胸前。

许多日子我温存服侍她。
我替她铺一个花床,我关上门不让强烈的光射在她眼上。
我轻轻地吻她的嘴唇,软软地在她耳边低语,直到她困倦得半入昏睡。
她消失在模糊的无边甜柔的云雾之中。
我摩抚她,她没有反应;我的歌唱也不能把她唤醒。

今夜,风暴的召唤从旷野来到。
我的新娘颤抖着站起,她牵着我的手走了出来。
她的头发在风中飞扬,她的面纱飘动,她的花环在胸前悉悉作响。

死亡的推送把她摇晃活了。
我们面面相看,心心相印,我的新娘和我。

O Death, My Death

Why do you whisper so faintly in my ears, O Death, my Death? When the flowers droop in the evening and cattle come back to their stalls, you stealthily come to my side and speak words that I do not understand.

Is this how you must woo and win me with the opiate of drowsy murmur and cold kisses, O Death, my Death?

Will there be no proud ceremony for our wedding?
Will you not tie up with a wreath your tawny coiled locks?
Is there none to carry your banner before you, and will not the night be on fire with your red torch-lights, O Death, my Death?

Come with your conch-shells sounding, come in the sleepless night.
Dress me with a crimson mantle, grasp my hand and take me.

Let your chariot be ready at my door with your horses neighing impatiently.
Raise my veil and look at my face proudly, O Death, my Death?

呵，死亡，我的死亡

你为什么这样低声地对我耳语，呵，"死亡"，我的"死亡"？

当花儿晚谢，牛儿归棚，你偷偷地走到我身边，说出我不了解的话语。

难道你必须用昏沉的微语和冰冷的接吻来向我求爱，来赢得我心吗，呵，"死亡"，我的"死亡"？

我们的婚礼不会有铺张的仪式么？

在你褐黄的卷发上不系上花串么？

在你前面没有举旗的人么？你也没有通红的火炬，使黑夜像着火一样地明亮吗，呵，"死亡"，我的"死亡"？

你吹着法螺来吧，在无眠之夜来吧。

给我穿上红衣，紧握我的手把我娶走吧。

让你驾着急躁嘶叫的马的车辇，准备好等在我门前吧。

揭开我的面纱骄傲地看我的脸吧，呵，"死亡"，我的"死亡"。

I Come to Praise You

With a glance of your eyes you could plunder all the wealth of songs struck from poets' harps, fair woman!
But for their praises you have no ear, therefore I come to praise you.

You could humble at your feet the proudest heads in the world.
But it is your loved ones, unknown to fame, whom you choose to worship, therefore I worship you.

The perfection of your arms would add glory to kingly splendour with their touch.
But you use them to sweep away the dust, and to make clean your humble home, therefore I am filled with awe.

我来颂赞你

用一转的秋波,你能从诗人的琴弦上夺去一切诗歌的财富,美妙的女人!但是你不愿听他们的赞扬,因此我来颂赞你。

你能使世界上最骄傲的头在你脚前俯伏。
但是你愿意崇拜的是你所爱的没有名望的人们,因此我崇拜你。

你的完美的双臂的接触,能在帝王荣光上加上光荣。
但你却用你的手臂去扫除尘土,使你微贱的家庭整洁,因此我心中充满了钦敬。

The Image upon the Altar

With days of hard travail I raised a temple. It had no doors or windows, its walls were thickly built with massive stones.

I forgot all else, I shunned all the world, I gazed in rapt contemplation at the image I had set upon the altar.

It was always night inside, and lit by the lamps of perfumed oil.

The ceaseless smoke of incense wound my heart in its heavy coils.

Sleepless, I carved on the walls fantastic figures in mazy bewildering lines—winged horses, flowers with human faces, woman with limbs like serpents.

No passage was left anywhere through which could enter the song of birds, the murmur of leaves or hum of the busy village.

The only sound that echoed in its dark dome was that of incantations which I chanted.

My mind became keen and still like a pointed flame, my senses swooned in ecstasy.

I knew not how time passed till the thunderstone had struck the temple, and a pain stung me through the heart.

The lamp looked pale and ashamed; the carvings on the walls, like chained dreams, stared meaningless in the light as they fain hide themselves.

I looked at the image on the altar. I saw it smiling and alive with the living touch of God. The night I had imprisoned had spread its wings and vanished.

龛里的偶像

用了几天的苦工,我盖起一座庙宇。这庙里没有门窗,墙壁是用层石厚厚地垒起的。

我忘掉一切,我躲避大千世界,我神摇目夺地凝视着我安放在龛里的偶像。

里面永远是黑夜,以香油的灯盏来照明。

不断的香烟,把我的心缭绕在沉重的螺旋里。

我彻夜不眠,用扭曲混乱的线条在墙上刻画出一些奇异的图形——生翼的马,人面的花,四肢像蛇的女人。

我不在任何地方留下一线之路,使鸟的歌声,叶的细语,或村镇的喧嚣得以进入。

在沉黑的仰顶上,唯一的声音是我礼赞的回响。

我的心思变得强烈而镇定,像一朵尖尖的火焰。我的感官在狂欢中昏晕。

我不知时间如何度过,直到巨雷震劈了这座庙宇,一阵剧痛刺穿我的心。

灯火显得苍白而羞愧;墙上的刻画像是被锁住的梦,无意义地瞪视着,仿佛要躲藏起来。

我看着龛上的偶像,我看见它微笑了,和神的活生生的接触,它活了起来。被我囚禁的黑夜,展起翅来飞逝了。

You Man of Riches

In the world's audience hall, the simple blade of grass sits on the same carpet with the sunbeam and the stars of the midnight.

Thus my songs share their seats in the heart of the world with the music of the clouds and forests.

But, you man of riches, your wealth has no part in the simple grandeur of the sun's glad gold and the mellow gleam of the musing moon.

The blessing of all-embracing sky is not shed upon it.

And when death appears, it pales and withers and crumbles into dust.

你这富有的人

在世界的谒见堂里，一根朴素的草叶，和阳光与夜半的星辰坐在同一条毡褥上。

我的诗歌，也这样地和云彩与森林的音乐，在世界的心中平分席次。

但是，你这富有的人，你的财富，在太阳的喜悦的金光和沉思的月亮的柔光这种单纯的光彩里，却占不了一份。

包罗万象的天空的祝福，没有洒在它的上面。
等到死亡出现的时候，它就苍白枯萎，碎成尘土了。

Must You Call Me?

Is that your call again?

The evening has come. Weariness clings around me like the arms of entreating love.

Do you call me?

I had given all my day to you, cruel mistress, must you also rob me of my night?

Somewhere there is an end to everything, and the loneness of the dark is one's own.

Must your voice cut through it and smite me?

Has the evening no music of sleep at your gate?

Do the silent-winged stars never climb the sky above your pitiless tower?

Do the flowers never drop on the dust in soft death in your garden?

Must you call me, you unquiet one?

Then let the sad eyes of love vainly watch and weep.

Let the lamp burn in the lonely house.

Let the ferry-boat take the weary labourers to their home.

I leave behind my dreams and I hasten to your call.

你定要叫我么?

又是你呼唤我么?
夜来到了,困乏像爱的恳求用双臂围抱住我。
你叫我了么?

我已把整天的工夫给了你,残忍的主妇,你还定要掠夺我的夜晚么?
万事都有个终结,黑暗的静寂是个人独有的。
你的声音定要穿透黑暗来刺击我么?

难道你门前的夜晚没有音乐和睡眠么?
难道那翅翼不响的星辰,从来不攀登你的不仁之塔的上空么?
难道你园中的花朵,永不在绵软的死亡中堕地么?

你定要叫我么,你这不安静的人?
那就让爱的愁眼,徒然地因着盼望而流泪。
让灯盏在空屋里点着。
让渡船载那些困乏的工人回家。
我把梦想丢下,来奔赴你的召唤。

Traveller

Traveller, must you go?

The night is still and the darkness swoons upon the forest.

The lamps are bright in our balcony, the flowers all fresh, and the youthful eyes still awake.

Is the time for your parting come?

Traveled, must you go?

We have not bound your feet with our entreating arms.

Your doors are open. Your horse stands saddled at the gate.

If we have tried to bar your passage it was but with our songs.

Did we ever try to hold you back it was but with our eyes.

Traveller, we are helpless to keep you. We have only our tears.

What quenchless fire glows in your eyes?

What restless fever runs in your blood?

What call from the dark urges you?

What awful incantation have you read among the stars in the sky, that with a sealed secret message the night entered your heart, silent and strange?

If you do not care for merry meetings, if you must have peace, weary heart, we shall put our lamps out and silence our harps.

We shall sit still in the dark in the rustle of leaves, and the tired moon will shed pale rays on your window.

O traveller, what sleepless spirit has touched you from the heart of the midnight?

行路人

行路人,你必须走么?
夜是静寂的,黑暗在树林上昏睡。
我们的凉台上灯火辉煌,繁花鲜美,青春的眼睛还清醒着。
你离开的时间到了么?
行路人,你必须走么?

我们不曾用恳求的手臂来抱住你的双足。
你的门开着。你的立在门外的马,也已上了鞍鞯。
如果我们想拦住你的去路,也只是用我们的歌曲。
如果我们曾想挽留你,也只是用我们的眼睛。
行路人,我们没有希望留住你,我们只有眼泪。

在你眼里发光的是什么样的不灭之火?
在你血管中奔流的是什么样的不宁的热力?
从黑暗中有什么召唤在引动你?
你从天上的星星中,念到什么可怕的咒语,就是黑夜沉默而异样地走进你心中时带来的那个密封的秘密的消息?

如果你不喜欢那热闹的集会,如果你需要安静,困乏的心呵,我们就吹灭灯火,停止琴声。
我们将在风叶声中静坐在黑暗里,倦乏的月亮将在你窗上洒上苍白的光辉。
呵,行路人,是什么不眠的精灵从中夜的心中和你接触了呢?

My Love in a Former Life

In the dusky path of a dream I went to seek the love who was mine in a former life.

Her house stood at the end of a desolate street.
In the evening breeze her pet peacock sat drowsing on its perch, and the pigeons were silent in their corner.

She set her lamp down by the portal and stood before me.
She raised her large eyes to my face and mutely asked, "Are you well, my friend?"
I tried to answer, but our language had been lost and forgotten.
I thought and thought; our names would not come to my mind.

Tears shone in her eyes. She held up her right hand to me. I took it and stood silent.
Our lamp had flickered in the evening breeze and died.

我前生的爱

在梦境的朦胧小路上,我去寻找我前生的爱。

她的房子是在冷静的街尾。
在晚风中,她爱养的孔雀在架上昏睡,鸽子在自己的角落里沉默着。

她把灯放在门边,站在我面前。
她抬起一双大眼望着我的脸,无言地问道:"你好么,我的朋友?"

我想回答,但是我们的语言迷失而又忘却了。
我想来想去,怎么也想不起我们叫什么名字。

眼泪在她眼中闪光,她向我伸出右手。我握住她的手静默地站着。
我们的灯在晚风中颤摇着熄灭了。

Let the Parting Be Sweet

Peace, my heart, let the time for the parting be sweet.
Let it not be a death but completeness.

Let love melt into memory and pain into songs.
Let the flight through the sky end in the folding of the wings over the nest.
Let the last touch of your hands be gentle like the flower of the night.

Stand still, O Beautiful End, for a moment, and say your last words in silence.
I bow to you and hold up my lamp to light you on your way.

让别离甜柔吧

安静吧,我的心,让别离的时间甜柔吧。
让它不是个死亡,而是圆满。

让爱恋融入记忆,痛苦融入诗歌吧。
让穿越天空的飞翔在巢上敛翼中终止。
让你双手的最后的接触,像夜中花朵一样地温柔。

站住一会吧,呵,"美丽的结局",用沉默说出最后的话语吧。
我向你鞠躬,举起我的灯来照亮你的归途。

The Would-Be Ascetic

At midnight the would-be ascetic announced: "This is the time to give up my home and seek for God. Ah, who has held me so long in delusion here?"

God whispered, "I," but the ears of the man were stopped.

With a baby asleep at her breast lay his wife, peacefully sleeping on one side of the bed.

The man said, "Who are ye that have fooled me so long?"

The voice said again, "They are God," but he heard it not.

The baby cried out in its dream, nesting close to its mother.

God commanded, "Stop, fool, leave not thy home," but still he heard not.

God sighed and complained, "Why does my servant wander to seek me, forsaking me?"

自称的苦行人

夜半,那个自称的苦行人宣告说:
"弃家求神的时候到了。啊,谁把我牵住在妄想里这么久呢?"神低声道:"是我。"但是这个人的耳朵是塞住的。

他的妻子和吃奶的孩子一同躺着,安静地睡在床的那边。
这个人说:"什么人把我骗了这么久呢?"
声音又说:"是神。"但是他听不见。

婴儿在梦中哭了,挨向他的母亲。
神命令说:"别走,傻子,不要离开你的家。"但是他还是听不见。
神叹息又委屈地说:"为什么我的仆人要把我丢下,而到处去找我呢?"

I Shall Never Be an Ascetic

No, my friends, I shall never be an ascetic[1], whatever you may say.

I shall never be an ascetic if she does not take the vow[2] with me.

It is my firm resolve that if I cannot find a shady shelter and a companion for my penance, I shall never turn ascetic.

No, my friends, I shall never leave my hearth[3] and home, and retire into the forest solitude[4], if rings no merry laughter in its echoing shade and if the end of no saffron mantle flutters in the wind; if its silence is not deepened by soft whispers.

I shall never be an ascetic.

热词天地

1.ascetic [ə'setɪk] *adj.* 禁欲的；禁欲主义的
2.vow [vaʊ] *n.* 誓言；郑重宣布
3.hearth [hɑ:θ] *n.* 灶台；炉边
4.solitude ['sɒlɪtju:d] *n.* 单独；孤独

我永不会做一个苦行者

不,我的朋友,我永不会做一个苦行者,随便你怎么说。

我将永不做一个苦行者,假如她不和我一同受戒。

这是我坚定的决心,如果我找不到一个荫凉的住处和一个忏悔的伴侣,我将永不会变成一个苦行者。

不,朋友,我将永不离开我的炉火与家庭,去退隐到深林里面,如果在林荫中没有欢笑的回响;如果没有郁金色的衣裙在风中飘扬;如果它的幽静不因有轻柔的微语而加深。

我将永不会做一个苦行者。

I Hunt for the Golden Stag

I hunt for the golden stag.

You may smile, my friends, but I pursue the vision that eludes me.

I run across hills and dales, I wander through nameless lands, because I am hunting for the golden stag.

You come and buy in the market and go back to your homes laden with goods, but the spell of the homeless winds has touched me I know not when and where.

I have no care in my heart; all my belongings[1] I have left far behind me.

I run across hills and dales, I wander through nameless lands—because I am hunting for the golden stag[2].

热词天地

1.belonging [bɪ'lɒŋɪŋ] *n.* 附属品，附件；属性
2.stag [stæg] *n.* 成年牡鹿
 hunt for 猎取……（通常指食物或毛皮）；寻找某人（某物）
 laden with 满载……
 leave behind 忘带；留下；丢弃；使落后

我要追逐金鹿

我要追逐金鹿。
你也许会讪笑,我的朋友,但是我追求那逃避我的幻想。
我翻山越谷,我游遍许多无名的土地,因为我要追逐金鹿。
你到市场采买,满载着回家,但不知从何时何地一阵无家之风吹到我身上。
我心中无牵无挂;我把一切所有都撇在后面。
我翻山越谷,我游遍许多无名的土地,因为我在追逐金鹿。

吉檀迦利 （冰心 译）

Dungeon

He whom I enclose with my name is weeping in this dungeon[1]. I am ever busy building this wall all around; and as this wall goes up into the sky day by day I lose sight of my true being in its dark shadow.

I take pride in this great wall, and I plaster it with dust and sand lest a least hole should be left in this name; and for all the care I take I lose sight of my true being.

热词天地

1. dungeon ['dʌndʒən] *n.* 地牢
   day by day 一天天地，逐日
   lose sight of 忽视；忘记；看不见
   take pride in. 以……为傲

地牢

被我用我的名字囚禁起来的那个人,在监牢中哭泣。我每天不停地筑着围墙;当这道围墙高起接天的时候,我的真我便被高墙的黑影遮断不见了。

我以这道高墙自豪,我用沙土把它抹严,唯恐在这名字上还留着一丝罅隙;我煞费了苦心,我也看不见了真我。